Mary Steele MacKaye

Pride and Prejudice

A Play Founded on Jane Austen's Novel

Mary Steele MacKaye

Pride and Prejudice

A Play Founded on Jane Austen's Novel

ISBN/EAN: 9783955630638

Auflage: 1

Erscheinungsjahr: 2013

Erscheinungsort: Bremen, Deutschland

@ Leseklassiker in Access Verlag GmbH, Fahrenheitstr. 1, 28359 Bremen.
Alle Rechte beim Verlag und bei den jeweiligen Lizenzgebern.

Leseklassiker

PRIDE AND PREJUDICE
A PLAY

*FOUNDED ON JANE AUSTEN'S
NOVEL*

By

MRS. STEELE MACKAYE

*NEW YORK
DUFFIELD AND COMPANY
1922*

Copyright, 1906, by
DUFFIELD & COMPANY.

Published September, 1906.

SPECIAL COPYRIGHT NOTICE.

This play is fully protected by copyright, all requirements of the law having been complied with. Performances may be given only with the written permission of Duffield & Company, agents for Mrs. Steele Mackaye, owner of the acting rights.

Extract from the law relating to copyright:

"Sec. 4996. Any person publicly performing or representing any dramatic or musical composition for which a copyright has been obtained, without the consent of the proprietor of said dramatic or musical composition or his heirs or assigns, shall be liable for damages therefor, such damages in all cases to be assessed at such sum not less than one hundred dollars for the first and fifty dollars for every subsequent performance as to the Court shall appear just. If the unlawful performance and representation be wilful and not for profit, such person or persons shall be guilty of a misdemeanor, and upon conviction be imprisoned for a period not exceeding one year."

PERSONS OF THE PLAY

MR. DARCY—(OF PEMBERLEY, DERBYSHIRE). "*Possessed of a fine tall person, handsome features, noble mien, and . . . ten thousand a year . . . clever . . . haughty, reserved and fastidious; his manners, though well-bred, were not inviting. 'Some people call him proud,' said Mrs. Reynolds, the housekeeper at Pemberley, 'but I am sure I never saw anything of it. . . . He is the best landlord and the best master that ever lived.'*"

MR. BINGLEY—(OF NETHERFIELD, HERTFORDSHIRE, DARCY'S FRIEND). "*Just what a young man ought to be; sensible and good-humoured, lively . . . such happy manners! So much ease, with such perfect good breeding . . . Also handsome, which a young man ought likewise to be if he possibly can.*"

COLONEL FITZWILLIAM—(COUSIN TO DARCY). "*About thirty, not handsome, but in person and address most truly the gentleman.*"

MR. BENNET—(OF LONGBOURN). "*An odd mixture of quick parts, sarcastic humour, reserve and caprice. He was fond of the country and of books, and from these tastes had arisen his principal enjoyments.*"

MR. COLLINS—(A COUSIN OF MR. BENNET, AND NEXT IN THE ENTAIL OF LONGBOURN ESTATE). "*A tall, heavy-looking young man of five-and-twenty. His air was grave and stately, and his manners very formal. His veneration for his patroness, Lady Catherine de Bourg, mingling with a very good opinion of himself and of his authority as a clergyman . . . made him altogether a mixture of pride and obsequiousness, self-importance and humility.*"

PERSONS OF THE PLAY

SIR WILLIAM LUCAS—(AN INTIMATE FRIEND AND NEIGHBOUR OF THE BENNETS). "*Formerly in trade in Meryton . . . he had risen to the honour of knighthood by an address to the King during his mayoralty. The distinction had . . . given him a disgust to his business, and, . . . quitting it, he had removed . . . to Lucas Lodge, where he could think with pleasure of his own importance, and . . . occupy himself solely in being civil to all the world.*"

COLONEL FORSTER—(THE COLONEL OF THE REGIMENT STATIONED AT MERYTON).

MR. WICKHAM—(AN OFFICER IN THE REGIMENT). "*Endowed with all the best parts of beauty—a fine countenance, a good figure, and a very pleasing address. As false and deceitful as he is insinuating.*"

MR. DENNY—(ANOTHER OFFICER IN THE REGIMENT).

HARRIS—(THE BUTLER AT LONGBOURN).

MRS. BENNET—(THE WIFE OF MR. BENNET). "*A woman of mean understanding, little information, and uncertain temper. When she was discontented she fancied herself nervous. The business of her life was to get her daughters married; its solace was visiting and news.*"

JANE—(ELDEST DAUGHTER OF MR. AND MRS. BENNET). "*She united with great strength of feeling a composure of temper and a uniform cheerfulness of manner. Her mild and steady candour always pleaded allowances, and urged the possibility of mistakes.*"

ELIZABETH—(THEIR SECOND DAUGHTER). "*Although not so handsome as Jane, her face was rendered uncommonly intelligent by the beautiful expression of her dark eyes. She had a lively, playful disposition, which delighted in anything ridiculous, with more quickness of observation and less pliancy of temper than her sister. There was a mixture of sweetness and archness in her manner which made it difficult for her to affront anybody.*"

PERSONS OF THE PLAY

LYDIA—(Their Youngest Daughter). "*A stout, well-grown girl of fifteen, with a fine complexion and a good-humoured countenance—a favourite with her mother, whose affection had brought her into public at an early age.*"

LADY LUCAS—(the Wife of Sir William). "*Not too clever to be a valuable neighbour to Mrs. Bennet.*"

CHARLOTTE LUCAS—(Daughter of Sir William and Lady Lucas). "*A sensible, intelligent young woman, about twenty-seven, . . . Elizabeth's intimate friend.*"

MISS BINGLEY—(Sister of Mr. Bingley). "*A very fine lady . . . but proud and conceited.*"

LADY CATHERINE DE BOURG—(Aunt of Darcy and Patroness of Mr. Collins). "*A tall, large woman, with strongly marked features, which might once have been handsome. Her air was not conciliating. . . . Whatever she said, was spoken in so authoritative a tone as marked her self-importance.*"

HILL—(the Housekeeper at Longbourn).

MARTHA—(the Maid at Mr. Collins's Parsonage).

ACT I
THE DRAWING-ROOM AT LONGBOURN

ACT II
THE ORANGERY AT NETHERFIELD
ONE MONTH LATER

ACT III
MR. COLLINS'S PARSONAGE AT HUNSFORD
THREE MONTHS LATER

ACT IV
THE SHRUBBERY AT LONGBOURN
ONE WEEK LATER

PLACE: ENGLAND   TIME: 1796

"In the novels of the last hundred years there are vast numbers of young ladies with whom it might be a pleasure to fall in love,—but to live with and to marry, I do not know that any of them can come into competition with *Elizabeth Bennet*."
—GEORGE SAINTSBURY. Preface to the Peacock Edition of "Pride and Prejudice."

ACT I

PRIDE AND PREJUDICE
A PLAY

ACT I

The drawing-room at Longbourn. At the back, wide glass doors open upon a terrace which overlooks an English landscape. It is winter, and coals are burning in the fireplace. On each side of the glass doors are rounded recesses with windows. On one side of the room a door opens into the library. On the other side is a door to the hall—the chief entrance of the house. The room is handsomely furnished in eighteenth century style. MR. *and* MRS. BENNET *are discovered sitting on either side of the table.* MRS. BENNET *is knitting—*MR. BENNET *reading.*

MRS. BENNET.
[*After a slight pause and laying down her knitting.*] My dear Mr. Bennet, did not you hear me? Did you know that Netherfield Park is let at last?

MR. BENNET.
[*Continues reading and does not answer.*]

MRS. BENNET.

[*Impatiently.*] Do not you want to know who has taken it?

MR. BENNET.

[*Ceases reading and looks up at her with an amused smile.*] You want to tell me, and I have no objection to hearing it.

MRS. BENNET.

[*With animation.*] Why, my dear, you must know Lady Lucas says that Netherfield is taken by a young man of large fortune from the North of England. His name is Bingley, and he is *single,* my dear. Think of that, Mr. Bennet! A single man of large fortune; four or five thousand pounds a year. What a fine thing for our girls!

MR. BENNET.

How so? How can it affect them?

MRS. BENNET.

My dear Mr. Bennet, how can you be so tiresome! You must know that I am thinking of his marrying one of them.

MR. BENNET.

Is that his design in settling here?

MRS. BENNET.

Design!—Nonsense! How can you talk so? But it is very likely that he will fall in love with one of them, and therefore you must visit him as soon as you can. Consider your daughters, Mr. Bennet! Only think what an establishment it would be for one of them! Sir William and Lady Lucas are determined to go merely on that account. Indeed you must go, for it will be impossible for *us* to visit him if *you* do not.

MR. BENNET.

[*Who has risen during this last speech and now stands with his back to the fire, facing* MRS. BENNET.] You are overscrupulous, surely. I dare say Mr. Bingley will be very glad to see you, and I will send a few lines to assure him of my hearty consent to his marrying whichever he chooses of the girls—though I must throw in a good word for my little Lizzy.

MRS. BENNET.

[*Sharply.*] I desire you will do no such thing! Lizzy is not a bit better than the others. She is not half as handsome as Jane, nor as good-humoured as Lydia. But you are always giving her the preference.

MR. BENNET.

Not unless she deserves it, my dear. But in this particular instance my poor little Lizzy is the only one who is unprovided for. Lydia and the others belong in the schoolroom, and you tell me that Mr. Collins has already spoken for Jane.

MRS. BENNET.

Oh, that odious Mr. Collins! I wish he had never come here. I wish I might never hear his name again!

MR. BENNET.

Mr. Collins odious! You surprise me! I thought that he had won your full approval.

MRS. BENNET.

[*Fretfully.*] Oh, well, since he had to be your cousin, and since you *will* not do anything about the entail, I suppose it will be a mercy if he does marry Jane. [*Half crying.*] But I do think, Mr. Bennet, it is the hardest thing in the world that we have no son of our own, so that your property has to be entailed away from your own wife and children, so if you should die, we may all be turned out of the house whenever this Mr. Collins pleases. [*In bewailing tone.*] He certainly does seem to have all the luck in the world. Here he has just got this good living from that grand Lady Catherine de Bourg.

MR. BENNET.

But, my dear, that will soon be *your* luck, as well. You forget that your daughter is to profit by it.

MRS. BENNET.

Well, perhaps. I don't know about *that,* but, [*With renewed excitement.*] I *do* know that it is too monstrous that after you are gone I shall be forced to make way for this man and live to see him master in this house!

MR. BENNET.

My dear, do not give way to such gloomy thoughts. Let us hope for better things. Let us flatter ourselves that I may be the survivor.

MRS. BENNET.

[*This is not very consoling to* MRS. BENNET; *and therefore, instead of making answer, she goes on as before.*] If it was not for the entail I should not mind it.

MR. BENNET.

What should not you mind?

MRS. BENNET.

I should not mind anything at all.

MR. BENNET.

Let us be thankful that you are preserved from a state of such insensibility. But it certainly is a most iniquitous affair, and nothing can clear Mr. Collins from the guilt of inheriting Longbourn. However, you know he is doing his best to mend matters. He has not only handsomely apologised for his fault, but he has now assured us of his readiness to make every possible amends by marrying one of the girls. Surely, my dear, you must acknowledge that this plan is excessively generous on his part.

Mrs. Bennet.
[*Dolefully.*] Well, I suppose it might be worse.

Mr. Bennet.
[*Cheerfully.*] Decidedly worse. With Jane so well settled, and a single man like Mr. Bingley in prospect, I think you should be quite cheerful.

Mrs. Bennet.
[*Excited once more.*] Mr. Bingley! We shall never know Mr. Bingley. Oh, Mr. Bennet, you take delight in vexing me. You have no compassion on my poor nerves.

Mr. Bennet.
You mistake, my dear. I have a high respect for your nerves. They are my old friends. I have heard you mention them with consideration these twenty years at least.

Mrs. Bennet.
Ah! You do not know what I suffer.

Lydia.
[*Bursting into the room, followed by* Jane.] Oh, that horrid practice! [*Looking back at* Jane.] Jane does so keep me at it. [*Throwing herself into a chair.*] La, I'm tired to death.

Jane.
[*Who sees that her mother is half crying, goes and*

stands behind her chair, puts her hand affectionately on her shoulder, and bends over her.] Does your head ache, mamma?

MRS. BENNET.

Of course my head aches. Your father is so teasing. I cannot persuade him to call on Mr. Bingley at Netherfield, so I suppose we shall never know him.

JANE.

[*Smiling.*] But you forget, mamma, that we shall meet him at the assemblies, and Lady Lucas has promised to introduce him.

MRS. BENNET.

I do not believe Lady Lucas will do any such thing. She has daughters of her own. She is a selfish, hypocritical woman, and I have no opinion of her.

MR. BENNET.

No more have I, and I am glad to find that you do not depend on her serving you.

MRS. BENNET.

I may have to depend on her after all, Mr. Bennet, since *you* will do nothing to help me. [*Fretfully to* LYDIA, *who has been yawning and coughing.*] Don't keep coughing, Lydia, for Heaven's sake! Have a little compassion on my nerves.

[LYDIA *pouts and looks unutterable things.*]

MR. BENNET.

Lydia has no discretion in her coughs. She times them ill.

LYDIA.

I do not cough for my own amusement, papa. Jane, when is your next ball?

JANE.

To-morrow fortnight.

MRS. BENNET.

[*Starting excitedly.*] Ay, so it is—and Lady Lucas does not come back till the day before. So you see it will be impossible for her to introduce Mr. Bingley, for she will not know him herself.

MR. BENNET.

Then, my dear, you may have the advantage of your friend, and *you* can introduce Mr. Bingley to *her*.

MRS. BENNET.

Impossible, Mr. Bennet, when I am not acquainted with him myself. How can you be so teasing?

MR. BENNET.

I honour your circumspection. A fortnight's acquaintance is certainly very little. But if *we* do not venture, somebody else will, and if *you* decline the office *I* will take it upon myself.

Mrs. Bennet.

[*As the two girls stare at their father.*] Oh, nonsense—nonsense! I am sick of Mr. Bingley!

Mr. Bennet.

I am sorry to hear that; but why did not you tell me so before? If I had known as much a week ago, I certainly should not have called upon him.

Mrs. Bennet.

[*Springing from her chair and throwing her arms about* Mr. Bennet's *neck.*] What! You have really called upon him? Oh, how good in you, my dear Mr. Bennet!

Mr. Bennet.

It is very unlucky; but as I have actually paid the visit—and as he will very likely return it at any time, and bring his friend, Mr. Darcy, with him—we cannot now avoid the acquaintance of Mr. Bingley and his party.

Mrs. Bennet.

Oh, my dear Mr. Bennet, I was sure you loved your girls too well to neglect such an acquaintance. [Mr. Bennet *deftly takes her hands from his shoulders. She stands looking fondly at him.*] Well, how pleased I am! And it was such a good joke that you should have already paid Mr. Bingley a visit and never said a word about it.

MR. BENNET.

Yes. Yes. Well, I must go to the library. [*He goes to the door, but stops for a moment.*] Now, Lydia, you can cough as much as you choose. [*He goes out.*]

MRS. BENNET.

[*Looking after* MR. BENNET.] What an excellent father you have, girls! [*Turns to the girls.*] I do not know how you will ever make him amends for his kindness, or me either, for that matter. At our time of life it is not so pleasant to be making new acquaintances every day. But for your sakes we would do anything. [*Looking about her.*] Where is Lizzy? Lydia, my love, where is your sister?

LYDIA.

Oh, she is out walking with Charlotte Lucas and that dismal Mr. Collins.

MRS. BENNET.

Lizzy—out walking with Mr. Collins? Why didn't *you* go, Jane?

JANE.

I had to practise with Lydia.

LYDIA.

I'm sure I would have excused you. But what is Mr. Collins here for, mamma? I am sure I caught Mr. Wickham and Colonel Forster laughing at him the day we went to Meryton. Why does papa have a cousin like that?

MRS. BENNET.

He really cannot help it. It is the entail, my love—[*Mysteriously.*] But I hope that all you girls will be very civil to him, Jane especially.

JANE.

I—mamma?

MRS. BENNET.

[*Embarrassed.*] Yes—my love.—You see——
  [*She is interrupted by the sound of laughter outside, and* ELIZABETH'S *voice.*]

ELIZABETH.

Very well, Mr. Collins.
  [MRS. BENNET *makes a sudden awed gesture of silence to the girls, who fail to understand.* ELIZABETH *enters by the glass doors. She is dressed in winter walking costume: a large hat,—fur-trimmed pelerine, and a large muff. She stops in the doorway and looks at* MRS. BENNET, *half puzzled and smiling.*]

ELIZABETH.

Well, what is it, mamma? What is the matter?

MRS. BENNET.

Nothing. Hush! What have you done with Mr. Collins?

ELIZABETH.

[*Laughing.*] Oh, Mr. Collins is safe! He has gone round to the library.

MRS. BENNET.

[*With a sigh of relief.*] How providential!

ELIZABETH.

[*Looking back.*] But I have brought someone else with me.

[MR. WICKHAM *and* CHARLOTTE LUCAS *come in gaily.*]

ALL.

[*Exclaiming.*] Oh, Mr. Wickham!

WICKHAM.

[*To* MRS. BENNET.] How do you do, Mrs. Bennet? This is indeed a pleasure. [*Going over to* JANE.] Miss Bennet, I am *so* glad to see you. [*Reproachfully.*] You were not with our party! [*To* LYDIA.] Why do you never come to Meryton, Miss Lydia? Mr. Denny is quite downcast.

LYDIA.

[*Pouting.*] La, Mr. Denny!

WICKHAM.

And many others beside him, Miss Lydia.

[LYDIA *giggles.* WICKHAM *returns to* MRS. BENNET.]

MRS. BENNET.

Well, 'tis an age since we saw you, Mr. Wickham. What *have* you been doing?

WICKHAM.

Colonel Forster keeps me so busy that I have no time for enjoyment.

ELIZABETH.

Yes, Mr. Wickham bears all the marks of an harassed and overworked man.

WICKHAM.

[*Bowing to* ELIZABETH.] Thank you, Miss Elizabeth. You have given me the very terms I needed. [*To* MRS. BENNET.] You see before you, Mrs. Bennet, an harassed and overworked man. Miss Elizabeth will bear witness that I was on my way to a business appointment when I yielded to temptation and went off for a walk with her and Miss Lucas and their irreproachable escort.

ELIZABETH.

And Miss Elizabeth will also testify that you yielded with the celerity and ease of long practice.

WICKHAM.

[*Laughing; to* ELIZABETH.] But in this case who was the tempter?

ELIZABETH.

Oh, I will admit that Mr. Collins was partially responsible.

[*All laugh.*]

MRS. BENNET.

Come, Lizzy, you have been talking to Mr. Wickham all the morning. Now, let some of the rest of us have a chance. [*Turning to* WICKHAM.] You must stay to dinner, Mr. Wickham.

WICKHAM.

I wish I might. That is indeed a temptation. But you know Miss Elizabeth has just reminded me of my duty.

MRS. BENNET.

Oh, nobody ever minds Lizzy!

WICKHAM.

Truly, I cannot to-day, Mrs. Bennet. It is too bad, but I am to meet Colonel Forster [*Smiling at* ELIZABETH] on important *business* at the Drake Farm.

MRS. BENNET.

Well, I am very sorry.

WICKHAM.

[*Hesitatingly.*] I might perhaps bring Colonel Forster in for a few moments on the way back—that is, if we return this way.

ALL.

Oh, yes, do.

MRS. BENNET.

Yes, indeed. Tell Colonel Forster we should be delighted to see him.

WICKHAM.

Thank you, I will. But now I really must be gone. [*Bowing brightly to* JANE *and* LYDIA.] Good morning.

[*To* CHARLOTTE LUCAS.] Good morning, Miss Lucas. You must let me hear more about those clever plans of yours. I am vastly interested in them. [*To* ELIZABETH.] Good morning, Miss Elizabeth. [*Laughing.*] You must try to temper your justice with mercy the next time I join you in a walk. [*Pausing, he looks at* MRS. BENNET, *who is standing between her daughters.*] Do you know, Mrs. Bennet, that you always remind me of one of my old schoolboy phrases. *Filiæ pulchræ!—Mater pulchrior!* Good-bye.

> [*He runs off laughing. He has only gone a few steps when* LYDIA, *who has been standing close to the door, runs out and calls to him.*]

LYDIA.

Oh, Mr. Wickham!

> [WICKHAM *turns and* LYDIA *runs up to him and whispers something in his ear.* WICKHAM *laughs, then shakes his finger at her, still laughing, and goes off.* LYDIA *stops outside and watches him.*]

JANE.

Really, mamma, I think you should speak to Lydia. She is too forward.

MRS. BENNET.

Nonsense! You are jealous.

JANE.

Jealous! Of Lydia?

MRS. BENNET.
Well, she is no more forward than any of you. All you girls are crazy about Mr. Wickham. [*Indulgently.*] But I can't wonder at it. He certainly is a most engaging young man. What were those French words he said to me as he went out, Lizzy?

ELIZABETH.
They were Latin, dear. He paid a very charming compliment to our pretty mamma. He said—The daughters are lovely, but the mother is lovelier. You know papa always says that you are handsomer than any of us.

MRS. BENNET.
My dear Lizzy, I certainly have had my share of beauty, but I don't pretend to be anything extraordinary now. [MR. COLLINS *enters.*] Oh, Mr. Collins, there you are.

MR. COLLINS.
[*Bowing profoundly.*] I do not find Mr. Bennet in the library, Madam. Do you know where he is?

MRS. BENNET.
Why, really, Mr. Collins, I can't imagine. Did you enjoy your walk?

MR. COLLINS.
Most assuredly, Madam. The beauties of nature, not only in the landscape, but also [*Bowing to* ELIZABETH *and*

Charlotte Lucas.] in the blooming countenances of my fair companions, made our expedition a peculiarly enjoyable one.

Mrs. Bennet.

Well, I am very glad of it, I am sure. [*To Jane and Lydia.*] Girls, we haven't told Lizzy and Charlotte the news.

Elizabeth.

What news, mamma?

Mrs. Bennet.

[*Looking at Charlotte with an ill-concealed triumph.*] Oh, nothing of consequence, Lizzy, only your father has just told us that we may expect a visit at any time from our new neighbour, Mr. Bingley, and that friend of his who is stopping with him.

Elizabeth.

Oh, Mr. Bingley! That will be entertaining. [*Suddenly with mischief she turns to Mr. Collins, who all through this latter conversation has been staring at Jane with solemn persistence.*] Do not you think so, Mr. Collins?

Mr. Collins.

[*Starting from his absorption.*] Eh? What? [*Pompously again.*] Excuse me, Miss Elizabeth, on what subject did you ask my opinion?

ELIZABETH.

I asked you if you didn't think it was a very pleasant thing to meet new neighbours.

MR. COLLINS.

Most assuredly, Miss Elizabeth, if those neighbours are possessed of those qualifications which redound to their own credit, and to the edification of their friends. Otherwise, as a clergyman, I must hesitate in my approval. [*To* MRS. BENNET.] You realise, I am sure, Madam, the caution which should ever be exercised where my amiable young cousins are concerned.

ELIZABETH.

Yes, mamma, you really should be cautious.

MRS. BENNET.

Nonsense! Why, my dear Mr. Collins, we have found out all about them. Mr. Bingley and Mr. Darcy are connected with some of the most respectable families in England.

MR. COLLINS.

[*In amazement.*] Mr. Darcy? Mr. Fitzgerald Darcy! My dear Madam, can it be possible that you are to be honoured by a visit from him? Respectable indeed! Why, he is the nephew of my noble patroness, Lady Catherine de Bourg. It is true that I have never yet had the honour of meeting him—but he frequently visits his aunt, and she has promised to bring him on some occasion to inspect my humble abode. I am surprised, indeed, by this civility on his part. [*Anxiously.*] I only fear there may be some mistake, for Mr. Darcy has the reputation of possessing a very natural pride of birth; but if your information is indeed to be relied upon, I think Lady Catherine would consent to my approval of this visit, provided my fair cousins will keep in mind the proper attitude of respectful humility which should be assumed toward a person of his superior station.

Elizabeth.

We will promise you, Mr. Collins, never for one instant to forget either Mr. Darcy's exalted position or our own insignificance.

Mr. Collins.

[*Looking at her with admiration.*] With that assurance, Miss Elizabeth, I think even Lady Catherine would be satisfied. So I need no longer withhold my sanction.

Elizabeth.

[*Curtsying.*] We thank you, sir.

Mr. Collins.

This is the very attitude of mind I could desire. [*To Mrs. Bennet.*] I think, with your permission, I will now retire again to the library. [*Going over smilingly to Jane.*] There was a volume of Fordyce's sermons that you may remember I was reading to you in this room yesterday. I do not find it in the library. Do you know where it is? [*Looking about him.*]

JANE.

I haven't seen it, Mr. Collins. I will try to find it for you. [*She starts as if to go out of the room.*]

MRS. BENNET.

[*Wishing to leave them together.*] No—no, Lydia will find it. Lydia, my love, go see if you can find the sermons for Mr. Collins.

[LYDIA, *with a grimace, rises slowly from her chair.*]

CHARLOTTE LUCAS.

Oh, Mrs. Bennet, I am quite sure that I saw the book in the hall. I will go fetch it.

MRS. BENNET.

[*Sharply.*] On no account, Charlotte. Lydia will find the book. Lizzy, go and get the mud off your shoes.

MR. COLLINS.

Oh, I will not trouble any of you ladies.

MRS. BENNET.

It is no trouble, Mr. Collins. Charlotte, if you will come with me, I have a parcel I should like to send your mother.

MR. COLLINS.

But I assure you, Madam——

    [*As they go out,* MRS. BENNET—*looking daggers at* CHARLOTTE—*tries to keep* MR. COLLINS *with* JANE.]

MRS. BENNET.

Lydia will find your book, Mr. Collins.

MR. COLLINS.

On no account, Madam——

    [*With awkward gallantry* MR. COLLINS *ushers out the ladies—*LYDIA *rebellious,* CHARLOTTE *somewhat offended.*]

ELIZABETH.

[*With an amused smile, having watched the party vanish, turns to* JANE *and speaks to her in mock-heroic fashion.*] Miss Bennet! Do you realise the honour which is so soon to fall upon our humble home, and our gratefully humble selves?

JANE.

[*Smiling.*] Oh, Lizzy!

ELIZABETH.

Do you really grasp in its full significance the fact that we may soon be honoured by a visit from Mr. Bingley of

Netherfield and Mr. Fiztgerald Darcy, nephew of the Lady Catherine de Bourg?

JANE.

Oh, Lizzy, Mr. Collins is a little pompous, but he seems a very well-meaning young man—indeed, sometimes quite agreeable.

ELIZABETH.

[*Looking quizzically, but affectionately, at her sister.*] No one can be anything but agreeable in the mind of our dear Jane. This time, however, I quite agree with you, I am as delighted as papa with Mr. Collins. I can see that his mixture of servility and importance promises well.

JANE.

And I think Mr. Bingley and Mr. Darcy promise well. If the half of what our neighbours say is true, Mr. Bingley will give us all sorts of gaieties. [*Slyly.*] Who knows? We may find him as entertaining as Mr. Wickham.

ELIZABETH.

As Mr. Wickham? Then, dear Jane, we shall be rich indeed. [*Counting on her fingers.*] For hospitality—Mr. Bingley; for conversation—Mr. Wickham; for grandeur—Mr. Darcy, and the agreeable Mr. Collins!

JANE.

Oh, Lizzy! Can not you let the poor man alone?

Elizabeth

With all my heart. I will gladly let him alone. You shall have him all to yourself. [*Mischievously.*] If only Mr. Collins knew your good opinion of him! But he is too modest to find it out for himself.

Jane.

[*Playfully pulling* Elizabeth's *ear.*] You are a tease!

Harris.

[*Entering.*] The two gentlemen from Netherfield have just brought their horses into the paddock, Madam.

Jane.

Show them in, Harris, and speak to Mrs. Bennet at once.

[Harris *bows and goes out.*]

Jane.

They have come soon, Lizzy. Really this is very civil in them.

Elizabeth.

Uncommonly civil. Come with me, Jane. I must make myself tidy. Mud and dirty petticoats for Mr. Darcy! —Oh, that would never do.

[*They run off, laughing. There is a short pause. Then* Mr. Bingley *and* Mr. Darcy *enter. The latter is very quiet, with an air of scornful hauteur.* BINGLEY, *on the contrary, has a gracious and animated manner.* HARRIS *ushers them in, much impressed.*]

BINGLEY.

[*To* HARRIS.] You will announce us to Mr. Bennet and the ladies.

[HARRIS *goes out.*]

Do you know, Darcy, I believe that was George Wickham we saw just now, going toward the Drake Farm.

DARCY.

[*Quietly.*] I think there is no doubt of it.

BINGLEY.

But what is he doing here?

DARCY.

[*With assumed indifference.*] Probably it is his regiment which is stationed at Meryton.

BINGLEY.

[*Excitedly.*] No, Darcy! You don't mean it! Why, confound it, if I had had any notion of that—I . . . I . . .

DARCY.

[*Contemptuously.*] I don't think we need mind Wickham.

BINGLEY.

But I do mind! To think that I should bring you into the neighbourhood of that rascal——

DARCY.

He must live somewhere, I suppose.

BINGLEY.

Yes, unfortunately. But, Darcy, you are a puzzle to me.—You are, indeed! How can you speak with any charity of a man who for years abused the patience and generous kindness of your father, and who so lately has attempted against your family the most dastardly action that——

DARCY.

[*Interrupting him with hauteur.*] We have already said too much of George Wickham. I prefer not to discuss him further.

> [BINGLEY *turns away hurt and embarrassed.* DARCY *seeing the effect of his words and manner, goes to him kindly, and speaks to him in a changed voice.*]

Bingley, I entirely understand your indignation. Indeed, I share it so fully that I dare not trust myself to think of the man's villainy. It is better that I say nothing of him, even to you.

BINGLEY.

[*Moved.*] I am sure, I beg your pardon, Darcy.

DARCY.

It is rather for me to ask yours.

> [*There follows an awkward pause, which* BINGLEY *at length breaks by speaking in a tone of forced gaiety.*]

BINGLEY.

Pretty place, this.

DARCY.

[*With a shrug.*] Very small.

BINGLEY.

What has the size to do with it? I think we are in luck to have such charming neighbours. You know we saw two of the young ladies going through the lane the other day. Why, Darcy, one of them is the most beautiful creature I ever beheld—and the other—the one with the dark eyes—she is uncommonly pretty. Don't you think so?

DARCY.

She is tolerable, but fine eyes cannot change family connections.

BINGLEY.

[*Quickly.*] What do you mean?

DARCY.

I think I have heard you say that their uncle is an attorney in Meryton.

BINGLEY.

[*Shortly.*] Yes.

DARCY.

And that they have another in London who lives somewhere near Cheapside.

BINGLEY.

[*With irritation.*] If they had uncles enough to fill all Cheapside, it wouldn't make them one jot less handsome.

DARCY.

But it must materially lessen their chances of marrying men of any consideration in the world.

BINGLEY.

Of marrying? You go fast, Darcy.

DARCY.

Perhaps. But I am in no humour to give consequence to young ladies. I am here to please you, Bingley—and— [*He smiles meaningly.*] knowing your disposition, I think it is just as well that I came.

[BINGLEY *is about to reply when the door opens and* MRS. BENNET *enters, followed by* JANE *and*

ELIZABETH. *The two young men make ceremonious bows.* MRS. BENNET *curtsies and then advances with delighted fussiness.*]

MRS. BENNET.

Good morning, gentlemen. I am so sorry that Mr. Bennet has gone for his walk.

[*As she looks a little puzzled from one to the other,* BINGLEY *advances.*]

BINGLEY.

Good morning, Mrs. Bennet. I am Mr. Bingley, your new neighbour at Netherfield. This is my friend, Mr. Darcy, of Pendleton, Derbyshire. [*All bow and curtsy.*] Mr. Bennet has been so kind as to call upon us, and we are most happy to have the honour of waiting upon the ladies of his family.

MRS. BENNET.

We are delighted to see you, I am sure! Mr. Bingley—Mr. Darcy—[*Indicating* JANE]—my eldest daughter, Miss Bennet. [*Indicating* ELIZABETH]—Miss Elizabeth Bennet.

[*The girls make low curtsies—the gentlemen bow.*]

Will not you be seated, gentlemen? [*The guests and ladies seat themselves.*] I am sure you must like Netherfield, Mr. Bingley. I do not know a place in the country that is equal to Netherfield. You will not think of quitting it in a hurry, I hope, though you have but a short lease.

BINGLEY.

Whatever I do is done in a hurry, Mrs. Bennet, and therefore if I should resolve to quit Netherfield I should probably be off in five minutes. At present, however, [*looking intently at* JANE] I consider myself as quite fixed here.

JANE.

It is very pleasant to have Netherfield open once more, although you must both miss London. There is so much gaiety in London.

DARCY.

Yes, in a country neighbourhood you move in a confined and unvarying society.
   [MRS. BENNET *looks vexed at this speech.*]

ELIZABETH.

But people themselves alter so much that there is something new to be observed in them forever.
   [DARCY *turns and looks at* ELIZABETH *with surprise and interest.*]

BINGLEY.

Then you are a student of character, Miss Elizabeth. It must be an amusing study.

Mrs. Bennet.

Yes, Lizzy always likes to watch people. [*Looking at* Darcy.] And there are plenty of people about, even if you do live in the country. The country is a vast deal pleasanter than London, is not it, Mr. Bingley?

Bingley.

When I am in the country I never wish to leave it, and when I am in town it is pretty much the same. They have each their advantages and I am equally happy in either.

Mrs. Bennet.

Ay—that is because *you* have the right disposition. [*Looking at* Darcy.] But that gentleman seemed to think the country was nothing at all.

Elizabeth.

[*Quickly.*] Indeed, mamma, you are mistaken. You quite mistook Mr. Darcy. He only meant that there is not such a variety of people to be met with in the country as in town, which you must acknowledge to be true.

Mrs. Bennet.

Certainly, my dear, nobody said there was—but as to not meeting with many people in this neighbourhood, I believe there are few neighbourhoods larger. I know we dine with four-and-twenty families.

[*As all become embarrassed at this speech,* Bingley *comes to the rescue.*]

BINGLEY.

Yes, there are many fine estates hereabout. Can you see Sir William Lucas' place from the garden? I am not quite sure I have placed it.

MRS. BENNET.

Oh, yes, there is a fine view of the chimneys from the terrace. Sir William is our nearest neighbour. Such an agreeable man—so genteel, and so easy—— [*Rising, she goes toward the glass doors.*] Come, Jane, we must show Mr. Bingley Sir William's chimneys.

    [MRS. BENNET, BINGLEY, *and* JANE *go out upon the terrace.*]

ELIZABETH.

[*Smiling mischievously.*] Would not you also like to see the chimneys, Mr. Darcy?

DARCY.

Thank you. Like yourself, I prefer people to places

ELIZABETH.

Did I say that?

DARCY.

Not precisely. But I have drawn that conclusion.

ELIZABETH.

[*Gathering her sewing materials, begins to embroider.*] Well, I can laugh at people better than places, and I dearly love a laugh.

Darcy.

Isn't that rather a dangerous trait, Miss Bennet? The wisest and the best of men may be rendered ridiculous by a person whose first object in life is a joke.

Elizabeth.

Certainly. But I hope I never ridicule what is wise or good. Whims and inconsistencies do divert me, I own, and I laugh at them whenever I can. [*Mischievously.*] But these, I suppose, are precisely what you are without.

Darcy.

Perhaps that is not possible for anyone. But it has been the study of my life to avoid those weaknesses which often expose a strong understanding to ridicule.

Elizabeth.

And in your list of weaknesses do you include such faults as vanity and pride, for instance?

Darcy.

Yes, vanity is a weakness, indeed, but *pride,* where there is a real superiority of mind—pride will be always under good regulation.

Elizabeth.

I am perfectly convinced, Mr. Darcy, that you have no defect.

Darcy.

I have made no such pretension, Miss Bennet. I have faults enough. My temper I dare not vouch for. I cannot forget the follies and vices of others against myself. My good opinion once lost is lost forever.

Elizabeth.

That is a failing, indeed. Implacable resentment *is* a shade in a character. But you have chosen your fault well. I really cannot laugh at it. You are safe from me.

Darcy.

There is, I believe, in every disposition a tendency to some particular evil—a natural defect which not even the best education can overcome.

Elizabeth.

And your defect is a propensity to hate everybody.

Darcy.

[*Smiling.*] And yours to wilfully misunderstand them. [*Voices are heard outside.* Elizabeth *applies herself to her embroidery.* Bingley, Jane, *and* Mrs. Bennet *return from the terrace.*]

Bingley.

The surrounding country is really charming, Mrs. Bennet.

Mrs. Bennet.

We think so. But you must give us a ball at Netherfield, Mr. Bingley, and then you will see that some of the people who live here are worth knowing.

Elizabeth.

[*Distressed.*] Oh, mamma!

Jane.

Mamma!

Bingley.

Certainly, Mrs. Bennet. I had already decided upon it. I told Mr. Darcy only yesterday that as soon as my sister, Miss Bingley, arrived, and Nicholas could make white soup enough, I should send out my cards. Did not I, Darcy?

Darcy.

[*Very stiffly.*] I believe you did.

Mrs. Bennet.

Well, that is vastly good in you, Mr. Bingley; and then, perhaps, your friend may change his mind about the country. [*To* Darcy.] You didn't come to admire Sir William's chimneys, Mr. Darcy.

Darcy.

I was admiring your daughter's work, Madam.

MRS. BENNET.

Oh, you should see Jane's work. Lizzy is all for books, like her father. She is a great reader and has no pleasure in anything else. Jane, show your embroidered parrot to Mr. Bingley.

JANE.

I do not think Mr. Bingley would be interested, ma'am.

BINGLEY.

[*Eagerly.*] Oh, indeed, I should, Miss Bennet; I am very much interested in parrots.—Pray show it to me.

MRS. BENNET.

Yes, and the new hand-screen. I will find it for you.
  [*All three withdraw, leaving* ELIZABETH *and* DARCY
    together.]

DARCY.

And so you are a great reader and take no pleasure in anything else?

ELIZABETH.

Mamma does not understand. I deserve neither such praise nor such censure. I am *not* a great reader, and I have pleasure in many things.

DARCY.

So I should have thought.

BINGLEY.

[*Looking at the screen which he holds in his hand.*] It is amazing to me how young ladies can have patience to be so very accomplished as they are; to think how you all paint tables and cover screens and net purses. It is quite wonderful.

ELIZABETH.

Do you agree with your friend, Mr. Darcy?

DARCY.

His list of the common extent of accomplishments has too much truth. But I cannot boast of knowing more than half a dozen young ladies in the whole range of my acquaintance that are really accomplished.

ELIZABETH.

Then you must comprehend a great deal in your idea of an accomplished woman.

DARCY.

Perhaps. To deserve the word, a woman must have a thorough knowledge of music, singing, drawing, dancing, and the modern languages. She must also possess a certain something in her air and manner of walking—the tone of her voice—her address and expression, and to all this she must yet add something more substantial—[*With a little bow to* ELIZABETH.] in the improvement of her mind by extensive reading.

Elizabeth.

[*Laughing.*] I am no longer surprised at your knowing only six accomplished women! I rather wonder at your knowing any.

Harris.

[*Enters and announces.*] Colonel Forster and Mr. Wickham.

[*The gentlemen enter, smiling.*]

Wickham.

Here I am again, Mrs. Bennet. I found that Colonel Forster had a message for the young ladies.

Mrs. Bennet.

I am delighted to see you. You are just in time to meet our new neighbours. [*Introducing the gentlemen.*] Colonel Forster, Mr. Wickham—Mr. Bingley, Mr. Darcy.

> [*As the gentlemen enter,* Mr. Darcy *has his back turned to them in conversation with* Elizabeth. *At the sound of* Wickham's *voice he starts and turns so that he faces the latter just in time for the introduction. At sight of* Darcy, Wickham *starts and is greatly confused.* Darcy *stiffens and scarcely nods when* Wickham *is introduced. The whole situation is so marked that everyone looks on with an astonishment to which* Mrs. Bennet *gives audible expression.*]

MRS. BENNET.

Well, well! If ever there was a proud, stiff man——

JANE.

[*In a dismayed whisper.*] Mamma!

BINGLEY.

[*Looking distressed, speaks hurriedly.*] Oh, Mrs. Bennet, I'm sorry that we cannot wait for Mr. Bennet. We—we—were on the way to meet my steward—and we are already late for the appointment.

MRS. BENNET.

[*Effusively.*] I am very sorry you must go, Mr. Bingley. But I hope you will come again. We must engage you soon for dinner.

BINGLEY.

[*In an absent and worried way.*] It will be a pleasure. [*Then with bows, the party moves toward the door.*]

MRS. BENNET.

[*Bustling.*] Your best way to the paddock is by the terrace.

  [*The gentlemen have almost reached the glass doors when* MR. COLLINS *comes in excitedly, putting himself directly in the way of* BINGLEY *and* DARCY.]

MR. COLLINS.

My dear Miss Elizabeth, I have this moment found out

by a singular accident that there is now in this room a near relation of my patroness Lady Catherine de Bourg. Will you present me?

[*He looks enquiringly from one to the other of the young men.*]

ELIZABETH.

Mr. Bingley, allow me to present my cousin, Mr. Collins—Mr. Darcy—Mr. Collins.

MR. COLLINS.

[*Taking almost no notice of* MR. BINGLEY, *he greets* MR. DARCY *with servile effusion.*] My dear sir—I trust you will pardon me for not having paid my respects before. My total ignorance of your presence here must plead my apology. [*Looking severely about him at the ladies.*] I was not informed of it. Is there any message, sir, which I could take from you to my honoured patroness—your aunt, or to your fair cousin—Miss de Bourg?

DARCY.

[*Stiffly.*] Thank you, I will not trouble you so far.

MR. COLLINS.

It would be no trouble—but an honour and a privilege.

DARCY.

[*Disgusted, turns from him to* BINGLEY.] We are already very late, Bingley.

BINGLEY.

Yes,—we have no time to lose.

[DARCY *and* BINGLEY *give passing bows and go out by the glass doors.* MR. COLLINS *keeps by* DARCY'S *side and, as they pass out of sight, is seen still talking to him, to his evident annoyance. All the time that the party is bidding good-bye to* BINGLEY *and* DARCY, WICKHAM *has been moodily standing by the fireplace.* ELIZABETH *has evidently been concerned about him, for throughout the foregoing interview with* MR. COLLINS, *she has looked at* WICKHAM *from time to time.*]

HILL.

[*Enters at the door leading to the hall.*] May I speak to you, Madam?

MRS. BENNET.

Yes, Hill, yes. [*To the gentlemen.*] Excuse me for a moment. I will return directly. [MRS. BENNET *and* HILL *go out.*]

COLONEL FORSTER.

Oh, Miss Bennet, Miss Elizabeth! Your aunt, Mrs. Phillips, has sent word by me that her card-party is to be on Wednesday. She hopes you will surely be there.

ELIZABETH.

[*In a pre-occupied way, looking towards* WICKHAM.] Oh, yes, we shall go.

COLONEL FORSTER.
[*As he passes the piano, and looking at some music which is on the rack.*] Ah! Here is the song you have promised to sing to me. Pray sing it now, Miss Elizabeth.

ELIZABETH.
Really, Colonel Forster, you must excuse me for to-day. Jane will play for you, instead.

JANE.
Indeed, I cannot, Lizzy.

ELIZABETH.
[*Looking meaningly at her.*] Please, Jane.

COLONEL FORSTER.
Oh, do, I beg—Miss Bennet.

[*All through the following interview between ELIZABETH and WICKHAM, the tinkle of the instrument is heard. During their conversation JANE'S back it turned—also COLONEL FORSTER'S as he looks over her music—so that ELIZABETH and WICKHAM are practically alone. ELIZABETH returns to her embroidery. There is an awkward pause for a moment. WICKHAM finally breaks it.*]

WICKHAM.
How long has Mr. Darcy been in Hertfordshire, Miss Elizabeth?

ELIZABETH.

Only for a very short time, I believe. He comes from Derbyshire, I understand, and has a very large property there.

WICKHAM.

Yes, his estate is a noble one. A clear ten thousand per annum. I am well informed on this head——[*Hesitates.*] I have been connected with Mr. Darcy's family in a particular manner since my infancy.

ELIZABETH.

[*Surprised.*] Indeed?

WICKHAM.

You may well be surprised, Miss Elizabeth, at this assertion after seeing the very cold manner of our meeting just now. [*After a pause.*] Are you much acquainted with Mr. Darcy?

ELIZABETH.

No. Though I have heard of him, I met him for the first time to-day, but even on this short acquaintance I should take him to be an ill-tempered man.

WICKHAM.

[*As if he had come to a sudden decision.*] Miss Elizabeth, you have been a witness of Mr. Darcy's treatment of me to-day, and therefore I feel that I must, for my own justification, acquaint you with the facts of my past connection with him.

ELIZABETH.

I shall respect your confidence, Mr. Wickham.

WICKHAM.

I am sure of it. [*After a short pause.*] Mr. Darcy and I were born in the same parish. My own father, who, to be frank, was steward of the Darcy estates, gave up everything to serve the interests of the Darcy family. Mr. Darcy's father was excessively attached to me:—indeed, I was his godson. He meant to provide for me amply, and thought he had done so. I was destined for the church and Mr. Darcy's father left to me a most valuable living. But the present Mr. Darcy chose to ignore his father's will and gave the living to another man. This closed for me the career for which I was most fitted and left me with almost no means of support.

ELIZABETH.

Good heavens! But how could that be? Why did not you seek legal redress?

WICKHAM.

There was an informality in the terms of the will which gave me no hope from the law. Mr. Darcy's father had relied implicitly upon the honour of his son.

ELIZABETH.

But—this is quite shocking. Mr. Darcy deserves to be publicly disgraced!

WICKHAM.
Sometime or other he will be, but not by me. Till I can forget his father, I can never defy or expose him.

ELIZABETH.
This feeling does you honour. But what can have induced Mr. Darcy to behave so cruelly?

WICKHAM.
I must attribute it in some measure to his jealousy. His father's uncommon attachment to me irritated him, but the fact is, Miss Elizabeth, as you can see, we are very different men, and he hates me.

ELIZABETH.
His disposition must be dreadful.

WICKHAM.
I will not trust myself on that subject.

ELIZABETH.
To treat in such a manner the godson—the friend—the favourite of his father! How abominable!

WICKHAM.
And yet, Miss Elizabeth, we must try to be just to him. Mr. Darcy has many good quaities. He can be both liberal and generous. He has also a brother's affection and pride which makes him a careful guardian of his sister.

ELIZABETH.

Oh, he has a sister?

WICKHAM.

Yes. You will hear him cried up as the most attentive and best of brothers. Oh, Mr. Darcy can please when he chooses. Among those who are his equals he is a very different man from what he is to the less prosperous.

ELIZABETH.

Contemptible!

COLONEL FORSTER.

[*Interrupting.*] Wickham!

WICKHAM.

[*Starting.*] Yes, Colonel Forster.

COLONEL FORSTER.

I fear we must be going.

WICKHAM.

[*Hurriedly to Elizabeth.*] Thank you for listening to me. It is hard to be misjudged.

ELIZABETH.

Thank you for your confidence. It is well to know the truth.

COLONEL FORSTER.

Well, Miss Elizabeth, I hope we shall see you all at your aunt's on Wednesday. Good morning. [*To* JANE.] Good morning, Miss Bennet. Thank you for the music. Please present my respects to Mrs. Bennet. I am sorry that we cannot wait longer.

WICKHAM.

[*Effusively.*] Yes, Miss Bennet, be sure to give your mother my best regards. Good morning—[*All bow and curtsy. As he is leaving he speaks aside.*] Oh, Miss Elizabeth, may I entreat——

ELIZABETH.

You may depend upon my sympathy.

WICKHAM.

[*Looking at her with an understanding smile.*] I am most grateful.

> [*The gentlemen go out of the door.* JANE *and* ELIZA-
> BETH *go into the recess and look from the window.
> There is a short pause.*]

MRS. BENNET.

[*Enters, flurried, and looks about her.*] Well, have they gone?

> [MR. COLLINS *enters through the glass doors at the
> center. He sees* MRS. BENNET.]

Mr. Collins.

Oh, Madam, I am just returned from attending on Mr. Darcy. Such a privilege! He was most condescending. I was able to tell him that Lady Catherine was very well on Saturday sennight. He is very like Lady Catherine. I am sure you must have been impressed by his distinguished manners.

Mrs. Bennet.

Well, really, Mr. Collins!
[A titter is heard from the recess where the girls are seated, and then Jane's voice.]

Jane.

Oh, Lizzy, hush!

Mr. Collins.

[Hearing this, turns and discovers the two girls. Then he speaks to Mrs. Bennet with lowered voice, as if an idea had just come to him.] This meeting is most opportune. Will you kindly step this way for a moment? *[He draws Mrs. Bennet aside.]* May I hope, Madam, for your interest with you fair daughter Jane, in the matter on which we were speaking yesterday? I would solicit the honour of a private audience with her this morning.

Mrs. Bennet.

Certainly, Mr. Collins. *[Hesitating.]* But there have been some changes since then. Some things have happened—I think it is right you should know, that—that Jane is very likely to be soon engaged. [*Encouragingly.*] But there is Elizabeth. I cannot take it upon myself to say—I cannot possibly answer—but I do not know of any prepossession in her case, and I am sure she can have no objection to listen to you.

[MRS. BENNET *goes to the fire and stirs it.*]

MR. COLLINS.

[*As soon as she has finished.*] Then Miss Elizabeth let it be, Madam. I was struck by her attitude of respectful awe when I mentioned the Lady Catherine de Bourg. Such modesty and humility of mind cannot but recommend her to my patroness.

MRS. BENNET.

[*Looking rather astonished at this last speech, but recovering herself.*] Yes, my daughter Elizabeth knows what is proper. She will be very happy to listen to you. Shall I call her now?

MR. COLLINS.

I think, Madam, there should be no further loss of time, as my leave of absence extends only to the coming Saturday.

MRS. BENNET.

Very well—[*She goes to the recess where the two girls are talking together.*] Jane, I want you upstairs. Lizzy, Mr. Collins has something he wishes to say to you.

Elizabeth.

[*Suspicious and dismayed.*] Dear ma'am, Mr. Collins must excuse me. I was just going away myself.

Mrs. Bennet.

Now, no nonsense, Lizzy! I desire you will stay. Mr. Collins has something *very* particular to say to you. [*As* Elizabeth *tries to escape.*] Lizzy, I insist upon your staying and hearing Mr. Collins. Come, Jane—[Mrs. Bennet *and* Jane *go out.*]

Mr. Collins.

[*Approaching* Elizabeth, *who does not move from the place where her mother left her.*] Believe me, my dear Miss Elizabeth, your modesty so far from doing you any disservice rather adds to your other perfections. But allow me to assure you that I have your respected mother's permission for this address. [*He escorts* Elizabeth *with clumsy gallantry to the sofa, then brings a chair and seats himself opposite to her.* Elizabeth *has recovered herself sufficiently to begin to enjoy the humour of the situation.*] My fair cousin, you must have at least surmised that I am about to ask you to become the companion of my life. And perhaps I had better begin by stating my reasons for this decision before I am run away with by my feelings on this subject. [Elizabeth *is so overcome with laughter at this idea that she can hardly speak, or keep a decent countenance.*]

ELIZABETH.

Oh, I beg, Mr. Collins——

MR. COLLINS.

One moment. My reasons for marrying are, first,—that I think it a right thing for every clergyman to set the example of matrimony to his parish; second, I am convinced it will add very greatly to my happiness; third, it is the particular advice of that very noble lady whom I have the honour of calling patroness.

ELIZABETH.

[*With more command of her voice.*] Believe me, Mr. Collins——

MR. COLLINS.

Excuse me—one moment. It remains only to be told why my views were directed to Longbourn instead of to my own neighbourhood. The fact is that, being as I am to inherit this estate after the death of your father (who, however, may live many years longer), I could not satisfy myself without resolving to choose a wife from among his daughters, that the loss to them might be as little as possible, when the melancholy event took place. This has been my motive, my fair cousin, and I flatter myself it will not sink me in your esteem.

ELIZABETH.

Mr. Collins,—I——

MR. COLLINS.

[*Rising and approaching nearer to* ELIZABETH.] Still one moment more! And now nothing remains for me but to assure you, in the most animated language, of the violence of my affection. To fortune I am perfectly indifferent, and you may assure yourself that no ungenerous reproach on that score shall ever pass my lips when we are married.

ELIZABETH.

[*Rising in her turn.*] You are too hasty, sir! You forget that I have made no answer. Accept my thanks for the compliment you are paying me. I am very sensible of the honour of your proposals, but it is impossible for me to do otherwise than decline them.

MR. COLLINS.

[*With another formal wave of the hand.*] I am not unmindful of the fact that sometimes a young lady's refusal is repeated a second or even a third time. I am, therefore, by no means discouraged by what you have just said, and I shall hope to lead you to the altar ere long.

ELIZABETH.

Upon my word, sir, your hope is rather an extraordinary one after my declaration! You must pay me the compliment of believing what I say. I wish you very happy, and very rich, and, by refusing your hand, do all in my power to prevent your being otherwise. This matter may be considered, therefore, as definitely settled.

[*She is about to leave the room when* MR. COLLINS *detains her.*]

MR. COLLINS.

One moment. When I do myself the honour of speaking to you *next* on this subject, I shall hope to receive a more favourable answer.

ELIZABETH.

[*Becoming angry.*] Really, Mr. Collins, you puzzle me exceedingly. I know not how to express my refusal in such a way as may convince you of its being one.

MR. COLLINS.

You must give me leave to flatter myself, my dear cousin, that your refusals of my address are merely words, of course. I shall choose to attribute them to your wish of increasing my love by suspense, according to the usual practice of elegant females.

ELIZABETH.

[*Very decidedly.*] Please do not consider me now as an 'elegant female'; I would rather be paid the compliment of being believed sincere. To accept your proposal is absolutely impossible. Can I speak plainer?

MR. COLLINS.

[*With awkward gallantry.*] You are uniformly charming; but I am persuaded that when my proposals are sanctioned by both your parents they will not fail of being acceptable. Meanwhile I may perhaps best serve my cause by leaving you to consider the matter by yourself for a while.

> [*He bows and withdraws to the door.* ELIZABETH *with a gesture as if she gave the whole matter up in despair, and yet half amused, goes to the fireplace. Just as* MR. COLLINS *reaches the door* MRS. BENNET *opens it.*]

MRS. BENNET.

Well, Mr. Collins, are we to congratulate each other? [*Looking doubtfully at* ELIZABETH.] Has all gone as you could wish?

MR. COLLINS.

I have every reason to be satisfied, Madam. My cousin has indeed steadily refused this, my first offer, and with considerable warmth, but this refusal would naturally flow from her bashful modesty. With your influence behind me, I have no doubt of my ultimate success.

MRS. BENNET.

Yes, you may depend upon me, Mr. Collins. I will speak to Lizzy myself directly. She is a very headstrong, foolish girl and does not know her own interest. But I will make her know it.

MR. COLLINS.

[*Alarmed.*] Pardon me, Madam, but if she is really headstrong and foolish, I know not whether she would altogether be a very desirable wife to a man in my situation. If, therefore, Miss Elizabeth persists in rejecting my suit, perhaps it were better not to force her into accepting me.

MRS. BENNET.

[*Alarmed in her turn.*] Sir, you quite misunderstand me. Lizzy is only headstrong in such matters as these. In everything else she is as good-natured a girl as ever lived. Let me see her alone for a moment. That will be the best.

MR. COLLINS.

But Madam—I——

MRS. BENNET.

[*Almost forcing* MR. COLLINS *out of the room.*] Oh, I shall very soon settle it with her, I am sure. [MR. COLLINS *goes out.* MRS. BENNET *goes quickly to* ELIZABETH.] Lizzy, what is the meaning of all this? Have you refused Mr. Collins?

ELIZABETH.

Yes, mamma, but please listen——

MRS. BENNET.

[*Angrily.*] No, I will not listen. I tell you what, Miss Lizzy, if you take it into your head to go on refusing every offer of marriage in this way, you will never get a husband at all. I am going at once to the library and speak to your father. You will listen *to him* perhaps.

>[Mrs. Bennet *starts to go when she sees* Mr. Bennet *outside passing the glass doors. He is just returning from his walk and carries a book under his arm.*]

Mrs. Bennet.

Oh, there he is now! [*She runs to the door, and opens it.*] Oh, Mr. Bennet—Mr. Bennet! [Mr. Bennet *turns.* Mrs. Bennet *runs out, takes him by the arm, and tries to pull him into the room by main force.* Mr. Bennet, *puzzled, submits.*]

Mrs. Bennet.

[*While she draws* Mr. Bennet *into the room.*] Oh, Mr. Bennet, you are wanted immediately. We are all in an uproar. You must come and make Lizzy marry Mr. Collins, for she vows she will not have him, and, if you do not make haste, Mr. Collins will change his mind and not have *her.*

Mr. Bennet.

I have not the pleasure of understanding you. Of what are you talking?

Mrs. Bennet.

Of Mr. Collins and Lizzy! Lizzy declares she will not have Mr. Collins, and Mr. Collins begins to say he will not have Lizzy.

Mr. Bennet.

Lizzy? I thought it was Jane.

MRS. BENNET.

No—no—It's Lizzy now!

MR. BENNET.

Ah! And what am I to do on the occasion? It seems a hopeless business.

MRS. BENNET.

Speak to Lizzy. There she is. [*Pointing to* ELIZABETH *at the fireplace.*] Tell her that you insist upon her marrying him.

MR. BENNET.

[*Turning to* ELIZABETH.] Come here, child. [ELIZABETH *goes to her father.*] This is an affair of importance. I understand that Mr. Collins has made you an offer of marriage. Is this true?

ELIZABETH.

Yes—papa—it—is.

MR. BENNET.

Very well—and this offer of marriage you have refused.

ELIZABETH.

I have, sir.

MR. BENNET.

We now come to the point. Your mother insists upon your accepting him. Is it not so, Mrs. Bennet?

MRS. BENNET.

Yes, or I will never see her again!

MR. BENNET.

An unhappy alternative is before you, Elizabeth. From this day, you must be a stranger to one of your parents. Your mother will never see you again, if you do *not* marry Mr. Collins; and *I* will never see you again if you *do*.

ACT II

ACT II

The Conservatory or Orangery at Netherfield. On one side, an archway, approached by two or three steps and hung with curtains, separates the Orangery from the ball-room. On the opposite side is a smaller archway with curtains, which are looped back, giving a glimpse of the drawing-room beyond. There is another door on the right. BINGLEY *is discovered directing two* FOOTMEN, *who are putting a bench in place.* DARCY *stands watching him.*

BINGLEY.

A little more to the right, Martin. That will do. Push those lights farther back—behind the trees. Yes, that is better. [*Looking about him.*] I think that is all. You may go. [*The men leave the room.*] Well, Darcy, do you approve of the arrangements? Have you anything to suggest? Any criticisms?

DARCY.

I have no criticisms for the *arrangements*.

BINGLEY.

[*Laughing.*] But you have for the *ball*. Yes, I know—still I was really obliged to keep my promise.

Darcy.

I am glad to find that a promise is with you an obligation.

Bingley.

Oh, come, Darcy! I understand. Set your mind at rest. I am going to London with you, although I must say I do not see the necessity for it. I think you are exaggerating the effect of any small attentions of mine toward Miss Bennet. However, we will cling together, and fly a common danger.

Darcy.

[*Coldly.*] Common danger?

Bingley.

[*Smiling.*] Yes, common danger! I, too, have eyes. Where will you match the wit and vivacity of Miss Elizabeth Bennet?

Darcy.

[*Quietly.*] She is indeed charming, and I admit that were it not for the inferiority of her connections, I might be in some danger. [*Very coolly and confidently.*] But they form, for me, an insurmountable barrier against any possible peril.

Bingley.

Love laughs at bars, Darcy! [Darcy *looks annoyed.*] No,—I won't! It really is not fair, since it is my fault. You would never have been put to this test if you hadn't been so good as to stay on here with me after that——

[*Stopping suddenly, and with an entire change from his former bantering tone, he says in a hesitating manner.*] Darcy, do you really think you should be silent about Wickham?

DARCY.

[*Haughtily.*] Decidedly! I do not choose to lay my private affairs before the world.

BINGLEY.

But the fellow is sailing under false colours. You do not know what the result may be. I really must speak of this again, Darcy, even at the risk of offending you. [DARCY *makes an impatient gesture.*] I am truly concerned at the foothold this rascal has already gained in the Bennet family. What he has failed to accomplish once he may succeed in again. These young ladies have no brother to defend them.

DARCY.

Neither have they the wealth to excite Wickham's cupidity. At any rate I do not wish to be the one to enlighten the neighbourhood. Besides, I understand that he has left Meryton.

BINGLEY.

Even so—I——[*He is interrupted by* MISS BINGLEY, *who enters gaily from the drawing-room.*]

MISS BINGLEY.

Ah! Here you are! [*To* DARCY.] Will you be so

kind? [*She holds out her arm for him to clasp her bracelet.*] Your sister Georgiana should be here, Mr. Darcy. [*To her brother.*] Charles, you should have insisted on her coming.

BINGLEY.
I am not in the habit of insisting with Darcy.

MISS BINGLEY.
[*Laughingly.*] Very true. [*To* DARCY, *who has at length succeeded in fastening the bracelet.*] Thank you. [*Looking about her.*] It is vastly pretty, Charles, but I am much mistaken if there are not some among us to whom a ball will be rather a punishment than a pleasure.

BINGLEY.
[*Laughing.*] If you mean Darcy, he may go to bed, if he pleases, before it begins.

MISS BINGLEY.
But, Charles, it would certainly be more rational if conversation instead of dancing were made the order of the day.

BINGLEY.
Much more rational, my dear Caroline, but it would not be near so much like a ball.

MARTIN, THE FOOTMAN.
[*Entering, to* BINGLEY.] Several of the carriages have

arrived, sir, and the guests will soon be entering the ball-room.

Bingley.

[*To the* Footman.] Very well. [*To* Miss Bingley.] Come Caroline, we must be at our post. We will leave Darcy to make up his mind whether he will join us later.
> [Bingley *and his sister disappear through the archway leading to the ball-room.* Darcy *does not follow them, but walks thoughtfully up and down the room. The sound of a voice is heard announcing.*]

The Voice.

Mrs. Long—the Miss Longs. [*A pause.*] Colonel Forster and Mr. Denny. [*A pause.*] Mr. and Mrs. Goulding. [*A pause.*] Mrs. Bennet—the Miss Bennets. [Darcy *stops in his walk and goes toward the ball-room archway—then he walks once more up and down.*] Mrs. King—Miss King. [Darcy *again moves toward the ball-room; he lifts the curtain, hesitates—looks in—then disappears.*] Sir William and Lady Lucas—Miss Lucas—Mr. Robinson.
> [*The music now begins, the stage is left empty. After a short pause,* Elizabeth *and* Charlotte *appear between the curtains of the ball-room archway.*]

Charlotte.

[*Peeps in—then enters.*] Isn't this pretty! Come in here for a moment, Eliza. I want to tell you something.

ELIZABETH.

[*Following her.*] Why *did* I promise to dance with Mr. Darcy just now! Why did not I have more presence of mind!

>[*They sit on the bench together while they talk; the guests, at the back, pass to and from the drawing-room and ball-room, and the sound of music is heard faintly.*]

CHARLOTTE.

I dare say you will find him very agreeable.

ELIZABETH.

Heaven forbid! That would be the greatest misfortune of all. To find a man agreeable whom one is determined to hate! Do not wish me such an evil.

CHARLOTTE.

I wouldn't be a simpleton, Eliza. You are angry because Wickham is not here, but I wouldn't allow my fancy for him to make me unpleasant in the eyes of a man of ten times his consequence.

ELIZABETH.

My *fancy* for Wickham, as you choose to call it, is simply my sympathy for a most ill-used man: also the relief of meeting with good manners and a good understanding after the insufferable pride of Mr. Darcy, and the stupid pomposity of that *dreadful* Mr. Collins! [CHARLOTTE *starts.*] Oh, my dear Charlotte, I have never thanked you half enough for helping us to endure that man. It was so good-natured in you to sacrifice yourself by listening to those interminable speeches of his.—I am more obliged to you than I can express. But oh, what a relief it is to know that he is really gone!

CHARLOTTE.
[*Who has listened to all this tirade in increasing embarrassment*] Oh, don't! Don't, Eliza! You are making it so terribly hard for me. But,—but I must tell you. —I am engaged to Mr. Collins!
   [ELIZABETH *is stupefied with surprise and looks at* CHARLOTTE *for a moment in silent and incredulous amazement. Then with difficulty she speaks.*]

ELIZABETH.
Engaged! Engaged to—to Mr. Collins! Oh, my dear Charlotte—*impossible!* [*Hopefully.*] You are joking!

CHARLOTTE.
[*With spirit.*] No, indeed, Eliza, I am in most serious earnest. Why should you be so surprised? Do you think it incredible that Mr. Collins should be able to procure *any* woman's good opinion, because he was not so happy as to succeed with you?

ELIZABETH.
[*Confused.*] Oh, no—no—of course not. And,—and

you must forgive all I have just said. I couldn't possibly have imagined——

CHARLOTTE.

[*More sweetly.*] No, Eliza, indeed you could not. [*She puts her hand on* ELIZABETH'*s shoulder.*] And we shall be friends still?

ELIZABETH.

Why, of course, of course, dear Charlotte. It was only the—the surprise. You know how fond I am of you. You know I wish you all imaginable happiness.

CHARLOTTE.

Yes, I am sure of it. You must be surprised—very much surprised, so lately as Mr. Collins was wishing to marry you. But, dear Eliza, when you have had time to think it all over, I hope you will be satisfied with what I have done. I am not romantic. I ask only a comfortable home, and, considering Mr. Collins' situation in life, I am convinced that my chance of happiness with him is as fair as most people can boast on entering the marriage state.

ELIZABETH.

[*In an absent manner.*] Undoubtedly.

CHARLOTTE.

[*Looking at Elizabeth affectionately and wistfully.*] And you will come to visit me sometimes? I could not bear to lose you, Eliza!

ELIZABETH.
[*Looking up, and patting* CHARLOTTE's *hand.*] Surely, Charlotte! [*Smiling.*] We are to be cousins, you know.

CHARLOTTE.
[*Cheerfully.*] Why, so we are!
[COLONEL FORSTER *comes from the ball-room.* LYDIA *and* DENNY *enter from the drawing-room.*]

COLONEL FORSTER.
[*Hurriedly going to* CHARLOTTE.] I am to have the honour of this reel, I believe, Miss Lucas.

CHARLOTTE.
Oh yes, Colonel Forster.
[*She goes out with* FORSTER, *leaving* ELIZABETH *alone, still seated.* LYDIA *and* DENNY *approach* ELIZABETH.]

LYDIA.
I think we are being treated abominably ill, Lizzy! It seems that Mr. Wickham has gone off on business somewhere, so he will not be here at all. [LYDIA *looks off toward the ball-room.*]

DENNY.
[*Aside to* ELIZABETH *significantly.*] I do not imagine his business would have called him away just now if he had not wished to avoid a certain gentleman.

LYDIA.
[*Suddenly.*] Why, Mr. Denny—I do believe the reel is

half over—I dearly love a reel! We shall miss it, altogether. Come! [*She drags* DENNY *off.*]

ELIZABETH.

[*Alone.*] Well! Well! The world is surely upside down. Charlotte and—Collins! *What* a match!

DARCY.

[*Approaching from the ball-room.*] Do not you feel a great inclination, Miss Bennet, to seize such an opportunity of dancing a reel?

[ELIZABETH *makes no answer.*]

Do not you enjoy the reel, Miss Bennet?

ELIZABETH.

[*Looking up.*] Oh, I heard you before, but I could not immediately determine what to say in reply. You wanted me, I know, to say—"Yes," that you might have the pleasure of despising my taste; but I always delight in overthrowing that kind of scheme. I have therefore made up my mind to tell you that I do not want to dance a reel at all; and now despise me, if you dare!

DARCY.

[*Smiling.*] I do not dare.

[MISS BINGLEY *enters from the ball-room with an officer. They talk together.*]

Colonel Forster.

[*Entering from the ball-room, and looking about him, sees* Elizabeth *and comes to her.*] May I have the honour, Miss Bennet?

Elizabeth.

I do not dance the reel, Colonel Forster.

Colonel Forster.

Oh, the reel is over. This is our dance.

Elizabeth.

Oh!

[*She goes off with* Colonel Forster. Darcy *remains where* Elizabeth *leaves him and watches her till she disappears into the ball-room. The officer bows and leaves* Miss Bingley.]

Miss Bingley.

[*Approaching* Darcy.] I can guess the subject of your reverie.

Darcy.

I should imagine not.

Miss Bingley.

You are considering how insufferable it would be to pass many evenings in such society. Indeed, I am quite of your opinion. I was never more annoyed. The insipidity and yet the noise;—the nothingness and yet the self-importance of all these people! What would I give to hear your strictures on them!

DARCY.

Your conjecture is totally wrong. I assure you, my mind was more agreeably engaged. I was meditating on the very great pleasure which a pair of fine eyes in the face of a pretty woman can bestow.

MISS BINGLEY.

[*Looking at him very meaningly and sweetly, speaks with coquetry.*] Indeed! And will not you tell me what lady has the credit of inspiring such reflections?

DARCY.

[*With great intrepidity.*] Miss Elizabeth Bennet.

MISS BINGLEY.

[*Taken aback.*] Miss Elizabeth Bennet! I am all astonishment! How long has she been such a favourite? Pray when am I to wish you joy?

DARCY.

That is exactly the question which I expected you to ask. A lady's imagination is very rapid: it jumps from admiration to love, from love to matrimony in a moment. I knew you would be wishing me joy.

Miss Bingley.

Nay, if you are so serious about it I shall consider the matter as absolutely settled. You will have a charming mother-in-law! Of course she will always be at Pemberley with you. Perhaps you might give her a few hints as to the advantage of holding her tongue.

Darcy.

Thank you. Have you anything else to propose for my domestic felicity?

Miss Bingley.

Oh, yes! Let the portrait of your uncle, the attorney, be placed next to your great uncle, the Judge. They are in the same profession, you know, only in different lines. As for your Elizabeth's picture, you must not attempt to have it taken, for what painter could do justice to those beautiful eyes!

Darcy.

It would not be easy, indeed, to catch their expression; but their colour and shape, and the eyelashes, so remarkably fine, might be copied.

Miss Bingley.

[*Sarcastically.*] Oh, I fear not—[Elizabeth *and* Colonel Forster, *with others, enter from the ball-room*—Mrs. Bennet *with* Lady Lucas *from the drawing-room.*] Here comes the fair one—[*Seeing* Mrs. Bennet.]—and mamma-in-law as well. I will not intrude on the family party.

> [*She goes off laughing and mingles with the guests.* COLONEL FORSTER *bows and leaves* ELIZABETH *with her mother.* BINGLEY *enters with* JANE *from the drawing-room. He sees* DARCY, *who is standing where* MISS BINGLEY *left him, and comes to him.*]

BINGLEY.

I thought this next dance was the one you liked so much, Darcy. Let me find you a partner.

DARCY.

[*Starting, as if from a reverie.*] So it is. Thank you—I have a partner.

> [*He goes to* ELIZABETH, *bows, and they go into the ball-room together.* MRS. BENNET *and* MRS. LONG *follow them.*]

BINGLEY.

[*Looking after* DARCY *with a smile, turns to* JANE.] You must be tired, Miss Bennet. I propose that we sit quietly through this dance. Do you agree?

JANE.

Yes, indeed. [*She sits on the bench.*] It will be very pleasant. [*Looking about her.*] How very prettily you have arranged all the rooms, Mr. Bingley.

BINGLEY.

I am so glad you think so. I feared they were rather inconvenient for so large a party.

JANE.

Oh, I find them delightful!

BINGLEY.

You are always charitable, Miss Bennet. It seems to me you always manage to see the best side of everything. I never knew you to say an ill word about a person or a place.

JANE.

[*Smiling.*] Oh, I fear that is not quite exact. I only try to see things in their best light, perhaps.

BINGLEY.

That is just it. The rest of us rarely try to see things in that way. So you see I have proved my case. You are too amiable.

JANE.

Not for to-night, Mr. Bingley. Everybody is of one mind to-night. There is but one point of view—you are giving nothing but pleasure.

BINGLEY.

[*Soberly.*] I wish it were so—but——[*With impulsive*

earnestness.] Dear Miss Bennet, I wish to tell you—I must tell you——

[*He is interrupted by the people coming in again from the dance.* DARCY *and* ELIZABETH *enter with* SIR WILLIAM LUCAS *and others.* BINGLEY *and* JANE *rise from their seats and walk slowly toward the back of the room.* DARCY *escorts* ELIZABETH *to a seat and stands by her. They are both silent for a moment.*]

ELIZABETH.

It is your turn to say something now, Mr. Darcy. I talked about the dance, and you ought to make some kind of remark on the size of the rooms, or the number of couples.

DARCY.

[*Smiling.*] I assure you I will say whatever you wish.

ELIZABETH.

Very well, that reply will do for the present. Perhaps by and by I may observe that private balls are much pleasanter than public ones.

DARCY.

Do you talk by rule then?

ELIZABETH.

Sometimes. One must speak a little, you know,—and yet for the advantage of some, conversation ought to be so arranged that they may have the trouble of saying as little as possible.

DARCY.

Are you consulting your own feelings in the present case, or do you imagine that you are gratifying mine?

ELIZABETH.

[*Archly.*] Both, for I have always seen a great similarity in the turn of our minds; we are each of an unsocial, taciturn disposition, unwilling to speak, unless we expect to say something that will amaze the whole room and be handed down to posterity with all the *éclat* of a proverb.

DARCY.

This is no very striking resemblance of your own character, I am sure. How near it may be to mine, I cannot pretend to say. *You* think it a faithful portrait, undoubtedly.

ELIZABETH.

I shall not decide on my own performance. [*There is a short silence; then, as if with an effort,* ELIZABETH *speaks.*] I am surprised not to see Mr. Wickham here to-night. I find that he is a great favourite with the officers. He has made many friends among them.

DARCY.

[*With great hauteur.*] Mr. Wickham is blessed with such happy manners as may insure his *making* friends; whether he may be equally capable of *retaining* them is less certain.

ELIZABETH.

[*Excitedly.*] He has been so unlucky as to lose your friendship, and in a manner which he is likely to suffer from all his life.

[*They are both silent.*]

SIR WILLIAM LUCAS.

[*Coming up to them all urbanity and smiles.*] What a charming amusement for young people this dancing is, Mr. Darcy! I consider it as one of the first refinements of polished societies.

DARCY.

Certainly, sir, and it has the advantage also of being in vogue amongst the less polished societies of the world: every savage can dance.

SIR WILLIAM.

[*Smiling.*] Do you often dance at St. James?

DARCY.

Never, sir.

SIR WILLIAM.

You have a house in town, I conclude.
[MR. DARCY *bows, but does not speak.*]

SIR WILLIAM.

I had once some thoughts of fixing in town myself: but

I did not feel quite certain that the air of London would agree with Lady Lucas.

[MR. DARCY *bows in silence again*—ELIZABETH *is amused.*]

SIR WILLIAM.

But I must not further interrupt you, sir! I only wish to tell you once more how highly gratified I have been by your superior dancing; allow me also to say that your fair partner does not disgrace you. It is a great pleasure to see you together. I must hope to—to have this pleasure often repeated, especially when a certain desirable event, my dear Miss Eliza, [*Glancing at* BINGLEY *and* JANE, *who are talking earnestly together at the back of the scene.*] shall take place. What congratulations will then flow in: but let me not interrupt you—you will not thank me, Mr. Darcy, for detaining you from the bewitching converse of that young lady, whose bright eyes are also upbraiding me!

DARCY.

[*Murmurs to himself.*] So! [*Looking earnestly at* BINGLEY *and* JANE, *he seems much impressed by what* SIR WILLIAM *has said.* ELIZABETH *notices this. Recovering himself,* DARCY *turns to her again.*] Sir William's interruption has made me forget what we were talking of.

ELIZABETH.

I do not think we were speaking at all. Sir William could not have interrupted any two people who had less to say for themselves. We have tried two or three subjects already without success, and what we are to talk of next, I cannot imagine.

DARCY.
[*Smiling.*] What think you of books?

ELIZABETH.
Books? Oh no: I am sure we never read the same, or not with the same feelings.

DARCY.
I am sorry you think so, but if that be the case, there can at least be no want of subject. We may compare our different opinions of them.

ELIZABETH.
No, I cannot talk of books at a ball—my head is always full of something else.

DARCY.
The present always occupies you in such scenes, does it?

ELIZABETH.
[*In an absent manner.*] Yes, always. [*Suddenly.*] I remember hearing you once say, Mr. Darcy, that you hardly ever forgave; that your resentment once created was unappeasable. You are very cautious, I suppose, as to its being created?

DARCY.
[*Firmly.*] I am.

Elizabeth.
And never allow yourself to be blinded by prejudice?

Darcy.
I hope not.

Elizabeth.
It is particularly incumbent on those who never change their opinion, to be secure of judging properly at first.

Darcy.
May I ask to what these questions lead?

Elizabeth.
Merely to the illustration of your character. I am trying to make it out.

Darcy.
And what is your success?

Elizabeth.
[*Shaking her head.*] I do not get on at all. I hear such different accounts of you as puzzle me exceedingly.

Darcy.
[*Gravely.*] I can readily believe that reports may vary greatly with respect to me; and I could wish, Miss Bennet, that you were not to sketch my character at the present moment, as there is reason to fear that the performance would reflect no credit on either.

Elizabeth.

But if I do not take your likeness now I may never have another opportunity.

Darcy.

[*Very stiffly.*] I would by no means suspend any pleasure of yours.

[Miss Bingley *enters from the ball-room. She comes directly to* Darcy *and* Elizabeth.]

Miss Bingley.

Oh, Mr. Darcy—would you be so good as to go to Charles? He wishes very much to consult with you about some of the table arrangements. You will find him in the dining-parlour. [*With exaggerated politeness to* Elizabeth.] That is, if Miss Bennet will permit you.

Elizabeth.

[*Carelessly.*] Oh, certainly.

[Darcy *bows and goes out.*]

Miss Bingley.

[*To* Elizabeth, *after a moment's silence.*] So, Miss Bennet, I hear that you are quite delighted with George Wickham. He must have told you all a pretty tale. As to Mr. Darcy's using him ill, it is perfectly false. I do not know the particulars, but I do know that George Wickham has treated Mr. Darcy in a most infamous manner. His coming into the county at all is a most insolent thing.

I feel very strongly on this point, Miss Bennet, as Mr. Darcy's interests are so intimately associated with our own. [*She watches* ELIZABETH.] We hope Miss Georgiana Darcy may some day be my sister. My brother admires her greatly.

ELIZABETH.

[*With indifference.*]   Ah!

MISS BINGLEY.

Yes, and therefore we resent these falsehoods and this presumption on the part of George Wickham. But, really, considering his descent, we could not expect much better. He has evidently forgotten to tell you that he is the son of old Wickham, steward to the late Mr. Darcy.

ELIZABETH.

[*Angrily.*] His guilt and his descent appear by your account to be the same. I have heard you accuse him of nothing worse than of being the son of Mr. Darcy's steward, and of *that,* I can assure you, he informed me himself.

MISS BINGLEY.

[*With a sneer.*]   Oh! I beg your pardon. Excuse my interference; it was kindly meant.

[*She goes out.*]

ELIZABETH.

Insolent girl! You are much mistaken if you expect

to influence me by such a paltry attack at this. I see nothing in it but your own wilful ignorance and the malice of Mr. Darcy.

>[FOOTMEN *now come in with small tables, which they place about the stage.* BINGLEY *comes in and directs them.* DARCY *follows him.*]

BINGLEY.

[*To* ELIZABETH, JANE, *his sister, and others who have entered.*] I thought it would be pleasant to have some of the tables here. [*To* JANE.] We must have places together.

>[*With some bustle, all seat themselves. At the table on one side are seated* DARCY, ELIZABETH, BINGLEY *and* JANE: *A little behind them are* MISS BINGLEY *with* COLONEL FORSTER, CHARLOTTE LUCAS *with an officer. At the table on the opposite side is* MRS. BENNET *with* SIR WILLIAM *and* LADY LUCAS. *Behind them are more tables at which other guests are seated.*]

LYDIA.

[*Entering with* DENNY, *much excited, goes to* MRS. BENNET.] Mamma, have you heard the news? Mr. Denny has just told me that the regiment is to leave Meryton, and go to Brighton! Good heavens! What is to become of us, mamma?

MRS. BENNET.

[*Sympathetically.*] Are they really going? Well, my love, it *is* too bad! I know how you feel. I am sure I cried for two days together when Colonel Millar's regiment went away, five-and-twenty years ago. I thought I should have broken my heart.

LYDIA.

I am sure I shall break mine. [*Coaxingly.*] Mamma, might we not *all* go to Brighton?

MRS. BENNET.

Oh, if we only could! But I fear your father will not hear of it.

LYDIA.

Oh, papa is so disagreeable! I am sure a little sea-bathing would set me up forever! Wouldn't it, Mr. Denny?

DENNY.

Surely, Miss Lydia. Oh, you must manage it in some way.

   [*They move off and take their places at one of the tables.*]

MRS. BENNET.

[*Looking after them.*] Well, Lady Lucas, it is hard for a lively young girl like my Lydia to be cooped up in a place where there is so little going on. However, [*Looking at* BINGLEY *and* JANE.] we are not likely to have it so very dull in the future. [*In a loud whisper to* LADY LUCAS.] You know what I mean—[*Nudging her and laughing.*] Jane and Bingley!

LADY LUCAS.

Ah! Indeed!

MRS. BENNET.

[*With importance and in a still louder tone.*] Oh, yes! It's quite settled. Such a charming young man—and Netherfield only three miles from Longbourn! And Jane's marrying will be a fine thing for my other girls. They will be sure to meet other rich men who will fall in love with them.

ELIZABETH.

[*Who has heard the beginning of this conversation, makes a pretext to go to arrange her mother's scarf and says in low tones.*] Oh, mamma! Be careful, I beg. Mr. Darcy can hear you!

MRS. BENNET.

What is Mr. Darcy to me, pray, that I should be afraid of him? I am sure we owe him no such particular civility as to be obliged to say nothing *he* may not like to hear!

ELIZABETH.

[*In distress.*] For heaven's sake, Madam, speak lower! What advantage can it be to you to offend Mr. Darcy? You will never recommend yourself to his friend by so doing.

MRS. BENNET.

That is enough, Lizzy! I think I can take care of myself. I never knew before that it was a crime to speak to one's friends about what everybody can see plainly enough, who has eyes in his head. [*Turning to* SIR WILLIAM.] Did *you*, Sir William?

SIR WILLIAM.

[*Smiling.*] Our friends usually have very sharp eyes for what is going on, Mrs. Bennet! [*Significantly.*] I have, indeed, sometimes expected that *you* would observe what has been going on in our own household of late.

MRS. BENNET.

[*Sharply.*] Going on? What *has* been going on, Sir William?

SIR WILLIAM.

[*With an important air.*] It is only this, Mrs. Bennet, that Lady Lucas and myself have to ask your congratulations on our very great satisfaction in the recent engagement of our daughter, Charlotte.

MRS. BENNET.

Charlotte! Engaged! Why, who in the world is going to marry *her?*

[SIR WILLIAM *draws himself up with offended dignity;* LADY LUCAS *bridles.*]

SIR WILLIAM.

The gentleman whom my daughter has honoured with her hand is your husband's cousin—Mr. Collins!

Mrs. Bennet.

[*Rising in rage and amazement.*] Mr. Collins! Marry your Charlotte? Good Lord, Sir William, how can you tell such a story! Do not you know that Mr. Collins is going to marry my Lizzy—or—or one of my other girls!

Lady Lucas.

Well, really, Mrs. Bennet!

Sir William.

[*Offended.*] What I have told you is quite true, nevertheless, Mrs. Bennet. The whole matter was settled before Mr. Collins returned to Hunsford. I am sorry we are not to receive your good wishes.

Elizabeth.

[*Hastily.*] Oh, but you *are,* Sir William! Charlotte has already told me all about her engagement, and we shall be most happy to welcome her as a cousin.

Sir William.

[*Mollified and with gallantry.*] Thank you, Miss Elizabeth! I am sure other congratulations will shortly be in order.

 [*He glances significantly at* Darcy; Elizabeth *draws herself up.* Sir William, *smiling, makes a little bow and then turns to the table, where he and* Lady Lucas *busy themselves with their supper.*]

MRS. BENNET.

[*To* ELIZABETH.] So Charlotte has told you, has she? I don't believe a word of it!

ELIZABETH.

Oh, mamma!

MRS. BENNET.

I am sure Mr. Collins has been taken in. Well, I trust they will never be happy together, and I hope the match will be broken off.

ELIZABETH.

[*Imploringly.*] Mamma!

MRS. BENNET.

[*Turning on* ELIZABETH *in a rage.*] And *you* are the cause of the whole mischief, Lizzy! I think I have been barbarously used by you all!

[*While this conversation has been going on, the other guests have been taking their supper.* COLONEL FORSTER *now rises with a glass of wine in his hand.*]

COLONEL FORSTER.

Ladies and gentlemen— [*The buzz of conversation ceases.*] Ladies and gentlemen, I should like to propose the health of Mr. Bingley.

ALL.

Mr. Bingley!

COLONEL FORSTER.

[*Raising his glass.*] To Mr. Bingley—may the pleasure which he has given us all to-night be but a foretaste of the future happiness which he will both *receive* and *give* in this community.

ALL.

Mr. Bingley—Colonel Forster!—Mr. Bingley!
[*All drink as* BINGLEY *bows.*]

SIR WILLIAM.

[*Rising.*] And may *I* be allowed to still farther express the sentiments of this community, by proposing another toast in which I am sure you will all join me with enthusiasm? [*Raising his glass.*] To the Master of Netherfield! May he retain that title from his present fortunate youth, to his future green and honoured old age!

ALL.

[*Drinking.*] Mr. Bingley! Sir William! Mr. Bingley!

BINGLEY.
[*Rising.*] Ladies and gentlemen! Friends!

ALL.

Hear! Hear!

BINGLEY.
I—I really cannot tell you how much I am touched by

the very kind words of Colonel Forster and Sir William! And—and I only wish that I deserved them.

ALL.

Indeed, you do!

BINGLEY.

[*Embarrassed and looking toward* DARCY, *who with folded arms, is staring at the ceiling.*] No, I do not. I—I did not like to speak of such a painful thing on an occasion like this, and so I have told no one of the fact that I am about to—to leave Netherfield.

ALL.

Leave Netherfield! Oh! Oh!

BINGLEY.

[*Still more ill at ease.*] Yes.—It is a very sudden decision, but—but important interests have made it necessary for me to—[*Lamely.*] to leave Netherfield.

SIR WILLIAM.

But only for a time, Mr. Bingley! Let us hope it will only be a—a *temporary* separation.

MRS. BENNET.

Why, surely, Mr. Bingley, you will be back again very soon.

BINGLEY.

[*In a dogged manner.*] No—no. I am afraid my returning at all is extremely uncertain. In fact, I—I expect to leave Netherfield *permanently*.

> [*Great consternation.* JANE *looks down.* ELIZABETH *looks at* DARCY. MISS BINGLEY *has a triumphant smile.*]

COLONEL FORSTER.

[*Incredulously.*] Oh, my dear Mr. Bingley!

SIR WILLIAM.

[*Solemnly.*] This is, indeed, a calamity.

MRS. BENNET.

[*To* ELIZABETH.[Good Lord, Lizzy, poor Jane! What——

ELIZABETH.

Oh, hush, mamma!

BINGLEY.

[*Looks again at* DARCY, *who remains perfectly calm through all this commotion. This time the sight of him seems to make* BINGLEY *somewhat angry, and he pulls himself together and speaks in a firmer tone and in a more cheerful manner.*] But, my friends, nobody knows what may happen. We shall undoubtedly all meet again sometime, and meanwhile, you must not let what I have said spoil your pleasure. [*The music is now heard again in the ball-room.*] There is the music. We must have another dance together.

[*There is a general movement among the guests. Those at the back of the room begin to go into the ball-room.*]

BINGLEY.
[*To* JANE, COLONEL FORSTER, *and others near him.*] Let us make up a set here; I think there will be room.

COLONEL FORSTER.
Capital idea!
[*The* FOOTMEN *remove the tables.*]

MISS BINGLEY.
Oh, yes, capital! [*With meaning, to* DARCY.] Do not you think so, Mr. Darcy?
[DARBY *bows stiffly, without speaking.*]

COLONEL FORSTER.
Miss Bingley, may I have the pleasure?
[*She bows, looks daggers at* DARCY, *and takes her place in the dance.*]

BINGLEY.
[*To* JANE.] Miss Bennet, will you grant me the happiness? [DARCY *gives him a look which* ELIZABETH *sees.*] The—the *final* happiness of my stay at Netherfield.

JANE.

[*Curtsies, a tremor in her voice.*] Thank you.

[*They begin to form a set with* MISS BINGLEY *and* COLONEL FORSTER, LYDIA *and* DENNY.]

DARCY.

[*Crossing to* ELIZABETH.] May I have the honour, Miss Elizabeth?

ELIZABETH.

[*Looking at him with frank hauteur.*] Thank you, Mr. Darcy, I am indisposed.

[DARCY *bows, reddens, and crosses to the other side of the room. The music begins. Amid embarrassed astonishment,* SIR WILLIAM *and* CHARLOTTE LUCAS *fill the quadrille set. As the dance commences,* ELIZABETH *and* DARCY, *standing at either side of the dancers, exchange a glance of the keenest pride and prejudice.*]

ACT III

ACT III.

The parlour of Mr. Collins's *parsonage at Hunsford. At the back of the room is an open door. This door leads directly into the garden, beyond which is seen, through an opening in the trees of the park opposite, "the prospect of Rosings"—the residence of* Lady Catherine de Bourg—*"a handsome, modern building on rising ground." A wide cottage window, also at the back of the room, gives a plain view of the passers-by. On either side of the parlour is a door, leading to other parts of the house.* Elizabeth *is discovered standing at the open door and looking up at some one outside who is evidently climbing the trellis.*

A Voice (*outside.*)
Is this the cluster you wish, Miss Bennet?

Elizabeth.
[*Mischievously.*] No, Colonel Fitzwilliam. Those are buds; the ones higher still. There—by the eaves.
  [Elizabeth *laughingly watches* Colonel Fitzwilliam *until he appears with a cluster of half opened roses, which he presents to her with a gallant air.*]

ELIZABETH.

[*Taking the roses and putting them in her girdle.*]
Thank you.

COLONEL FITZWILLIAM.

May not I have *one*, as my reward, Miss Bennet?

ELIZABETH.

Is not accomplishment its own reward?

COLONEL FITZWILLIAM.

And is not the power to be generous the highest reward that can be given to any accomplishment?

ELIZABETH.

Oh, surely! And so *you* would have to be generous and get me some more roses: then we should each of us have to invent new speeches, and so we should never be done till we were ready to print a phrase book. However, you have certainly won your rose. [*She gives it to him.*]

COLONEL FITZWILLIAM.

Thank you! That phrase-book is a capital idea, Miss Bennet. Nothing could please me better than just such an occupation. It would really be a charity, for Darcy is such a dull fellow these days that I really don't know what to do with myself.

ELIZABETH.

But we should hardly have the time for such a project.

You say that you and Mr. Darcy are to leave Lady Catherine on Saturday.

Colonel Fitzwilliam.

Yes, if Darcy doesn't put it off again. He has already paid our aunt a much longer visit than ever before. I am at his disposal, you know. He arranges the business just as he pleases.

Elizabeth.

I do not know anybody who seems more to enjoy the power of doing what he pleases than Mr. Darcy.

Colonel Fitzwilliam.

He likes to have his own way very well, but so do we all. It is only that he has better means of having it than many others. [*Looking at his watch.*] I suppose I ought to go and look for him now. I expected to find him here, [*With a meaning smile.*] as not unfrequently happens. But since he is not, he probably expects me to meet him at the Crossroads.

Elizabeth.

I imagine your cousin brought you down with him chiefly for the sake of having somebody at his disposal. I wonder he does not marry to secure a lasting convenience of that kind. But perhaps his sister does as well for the present,—and, as she is under his sole care, he may do what he likes with her.

Colonel Fitzwilliam.

No—that is an advantage which he must share with me. I am joined with him in the guardianship of Miss Darcy.

Elizabeth.

Are you, indeed? And pray what sort of a guardian do you make? Does your charge give you much trouble? Young ladies of her age are sometimes a little difficult to manage. And, if she has the true Darcy spirit, she may like to have her own way.

[Colonel Fitzwilliam *looks at* Elizabeth *very suspiciously as she makes this last remark.*]

Colonel Fitzwilliam.

Why—what?—Why do you suppose Miss Darcy is likely to give us any uneasiness, Miss Bennet?

Elizabeth.

[*Carelessly.*] Oh, nothing at all! You need not be frightened! I never heard any harm of her; she is a great favourite with a lady of my acquaintance—Miss Bingley. I think I have heard you say that you knew Miss Bingley.

Colonel Fitzwilliam.

I know her a little. Her brother is a pleasant, gentlemanlike man. He is a great friend of Darcy's.

Elizabeth.

Oh, yes. Mr. Darcy is uncommonly kind to Mr. Bingley and takes a prodigious deal of care of him.

Colonel Fitzwilliam.

Care of him? Yes, I really believe Darcy does take care of him. From something he has told me, I have reason to think Bingley very much indebted to him. [*Stopping.*] But I ought to beg his pardon, for I have no right to suppose that Bingley was the person meant.

Elizabeth.

[*Curiously, and with ill-concealed anxiety.*] What is it you mean?

Colonel Fitzwilliam.

It is a circumstance which, of course, Darcy could not wish to be generally known, because if it were to get round to the lady's family it would be an unpleasant thing.

Elizabeth.

You may depend upon my not mentioning it.

Colonel Fitzwilliam.

And, remember, that I haven't much reason for supposing it to be Bingley. What he told me was merely this: that he congratulated himself on having lately saved a friend from the inconveniences of a most imprudent marriage, but without names or any other particulars, and I only suspected it to be Bingley from believing him to be the kind of young man to get into a scrape of that sort.

Elizabeth.

[*Trying to suppress her feeling.*] Did Mr. Darcy give you his reasons for this interference?

Colonel Fitzwilliam.
I understood that there were some very strong objections against the lady.

Elizabeth.
Indeed! [*Trying to speak calmly.*] And what arts did he use to separate them?

Colonel Fitzwilliam.
[*Smiling.*] He did not talk to me of his own arts. He only told *me*, what I have now told *you*.

Elizabeth.
Why was your cousin to be the judge?

Colonel Fitzwilliam.
You are rather disposed to call his interference officious?

Elizabeth.
[*Growing excited.*] I do not see what right Mr. Darcy had to decide on the propriety of his friend's inclination; why, upon his *own* judgment alone, Mr. Darcy was to determine in what manner his friend was to be happy. [*Recovering herself.*] But as we know none of the particulars, it is not fair to condemn him. It is not to be supposed that there was much affection in the case.

Colonel Fitzwilliam.
That is not an unnatural surmise, and I believe Darcy

told me that he did not think that the lady, at least, was very deeply concerned in the matter. However, to lessen the affection on either side is to lessen the honour of my cousin's triumph very sadly.

ELIZABETH.

Your cousin's triumph——
 [*Greatly excited, she is about to continue, when* CHARLOTTE'S *voice is heard outside.*]

CHARLOTTE.

Yes, Mr. Darcy, I think I saw Colonel Fitzwilliam go up the garden path a few moments ago. [*Protesting.*] Oh, no, Mr. Darcy, you are too kind! Really——

DARCY.

[*Outside.*] Pray, allow me.
 [CHARLOTTE *enters, accompanied by* DARCY, *who is carrying a basket of eggs. She wears a garden hat and gloves.*]

CHARLOTTE.

Ah, here he is. Good morning, Colonel Fitzwilliam. [*To* DARCY.] Pray let me have the basket now, Mr. Darcy. [DARCY *gives* CHARLOTTE *the basket, and then turns to* ELIZABETH.]

DARCY.

Good morning, Miss Bennet. [ELIZABETH *returns* DARCY'S *greeting with a self-consciousness which does not*

escape his notice, but the motive of which he mistakes.
DARCY *gives a quick glance from* ELIZABETH *to* COLONEL
FITZWILLIAM, *as he turns to speak to the latter.*] Ah,
Fitzwilliam, I thought I might find you here.

COLONEL FITZWILLIAM.
[*Lightly.*] Yes, I have been so fortunate as to secure some of Mrs. Collins's early roses for Miss Bennet.

CHARLOTTE.
[*In surprise.*] Really! Have they already opened?

ELIZABETH.
[*Who has by this time recovered her self-possession.*] A very few of them. But Colonel Fitzwilliam was obliged to climb very near to the sun to get me these. [*She looks admiringly upon the flowers as she speaks.*]

COLONEL FITZWILLIAM.
[*Showing the rose which* ELIZABETH *has given him.*] And you see I have my reward.

DARCY.
[*Smiling faintly.*] Colonel Fitzwilliam might not have won his prize so easily, Miss Bennet, had there been others in the field.

ELIZABETH.
Ah, no, Mr. Darcy, I cannot lessen Colonel Fitzwilliam's achievement by admitting any such possibility.

COLONEL FITZWILLIAM.
[*Gallantly.*] Thank you, Miss Bennet!
[DARCY *turns away with an unconscious look of chagrin.*]

CHARLOTTE.
Well, surely, my roses will have to bloom their prettiest this season in return for all the attention they have received. [*To the young men.*] Will not you be seated, gentlemen?

DARCY.
[*Tartly.*] Thanks, no, Mrs. Collins; I merely stopped for Colonel Fitzwilliam; but perhaps his rose-gathering has caused him to abandon our project of taking a walk together this morning.

COLONEL FITZWILLIAM.
By no means, Darcy, that pleasure has only been deferred.

DARCY.
Very good then. We will go at once, if Mrs. Collins and Miss Bennet will pardon me this hasty call.

CHARLOTTE.
Certainly, Mr. Darcy! [ELIZABETH *also, absent-mindedly, murmurs her assent, for which* DARCY *lingers with vague uneasiness before departing with* FITZWILLIAM. CHARLOTTE *looks at* ELIZABETH *curiously, then calls to the little maid, who enters.*]

CHARLOTTE.

Martha—take these eggs to the pantry. Do not disturb them.

MARTHA.

Very well, ma'am.
[*She curtsies and goes out.*]

CHARLOTTE.

[*Taking off her hat and gloves.*] Now, Eliza, we must get to our work and have a comfortable chat. You have been here nearly two weeks and we really haven't had a good talk yet.

ELIZABETH.

[*Getting out her embroidery.*] Yes, you promised me a quiet visit, Charlotte. But I find you are more lively here than we are at Longbourn.
[*The two ladies sit at the table with their embroidery.*]

CHARLOTTE.

But how could I have anticipated the arrival here of two very attentive young gentlemen? [*Smiling at* ELIZABETH.] It is really quite a surprising coincidence, or else Mr. Darcy has timed his visit to his aunt very cleverly. As to these daily visits to the parsonage—you may be sure I do not take to myself the credit of them. Neither of these young gentlemen would ever come so often to see me. I have to thank you, Eliza, for this civility.

ELIZABETH.

[*With a little temper.*] You may thank a lack of occupation on their part. You know very well my opinion of Mr. Darcy!

CHARLOTTE.

Yes. You have often expressed it. I wish I were as well informed of Mr. Darcy's opinion of Eliza.

ELIZABETH.

When you know the one, you know the other. They are identical.

CHARLOTTE.

Well, perhaps under the circumstances, that is the most satisfactory condition of things. And do we hold the same opinion of Colonel Fitzwilliam?

ELIZABETH.

[*Tossing her head.*] Oh, Colonel Fitzwilliam!

CHARLOTTE.

[*Looking at* ELIZABETH *sharply, and after a short silence.*] And so Jane is once more at home after her visit in London, and Lydia has gone to Brighton after all. How did she ever manage to persuade your father?

ELIZABETH.

Oh, Lydia was so determined upon it that she and mamma gave my father no peace till they had teased him to consent. But I am very sorry. Lydia is too foolish, too ignorant and wilful to be trusted away from home. I only hope that no harm will come of it.

CHARLOTTE.
And is Mr. Wickham still with the regiment?

ELIZABETH.
Yes, he went with it to Brighton.

CHARLOTTE.
I hear that he is thinking of marrying Miss King, since she has just received a legacy of ten thousand pounds. I should be sorry to think that our friend was mercenary.

ELIZABETH.
A man in distressed circumstances has not time for all those elegant decorums which other people may observe. If Miss King does not object to it, why should we?

CHARLOTTE.
Her not objecting does not justify—him.

ELIZABETH.
[*Emphatically.*] Well, have it as you choose. *He* shall be mercenary, and *she* shall be foolish! Mr. Wickham's worst fault, after all, is his power of being agreeable. Thank heaven, we both of us know some men who haven't one agreeable quality. Stupid men are the only ones worth knowing!

CHARLOTTE.
[*Smiling.*] Well, well, Eliza! That speech savours a little of—disappointment.

ELIZABETH.
Oh, yes—anything you please!

CHARLOTTE.
[*Changing the subject.*] And you say that Jane is not in her usual spirits?

ELIZABETH.
[*Shortly.*] Yes.

CHARLOTTE.
And she is looking poorly?

ELIZABETH.
[*Still more shortly.*] Yes—very!

CHARLOTTE.
Did she see much of the Bingleys in London?

ELIZABETH.
[*Bursting out hotly.*] She saw nothing of them. Oh, Charlotte, I have just had all my suspicions verified.

CHARLOTTE.
Your suspicions?

ELIZABETH.
Yes, there has been an arrangement in all this. Mr.

Bingley has been kept away from Jane by——[*Stops suddenly.*]

CHARLOTTE.

[*Looks up curiously, then speaks quickly.*] Don't imagine any such nonsense, Eliza. A young man like Mr. Bingley so easily falls in love with a pretty girl for a few weeks—and, when accident separates them, so easily forgets her, that this sort of inconstancy is very frequent.

ELIZABETH.

We do not suffer from accident, Charlotte. A young man of independent fortune does not suddenly decide of his own free will to think no more of a girl with whom he was violently in love.

CHARLOTTE.

But were they so violently in love?

ELIZABETH.

Yes—I never saw a more promising inclination. Why, Mr. Bingley would talk to no one else—would look at no one else. Is not general incivility the very essence of love?

CHARLOTTE.

[*Smiling.*] It is usually a good test. But if Jane did not return his affection— It really did not seem to me that there was anything *violent* in Jane's attitude. I could never see that she showed any extreme affection for Bingley.

ELIZABETH.

[*Hotly.*] Well, I know that Jane was very much in love with him, and that she showed her affection as much as her nature would allow. If Bingley didn't see it he must have been a simpleton. No—the real trouble was that Jane didn't see him often enough, perhaps, to make her understand his character.

CHARLOTTE.

Oh, if Jane were married to Bingley to-morrow, I should think she had as good a chance of happiness as if she were studying him for a twelve-month. It is far better to know as little as possible of the person with whom you are to pass your life.

ELIZABETH.

[*Demurely.*] In some cases that is undoubtedly true.

MR. COLLINS.

[*Appears at the garden door. He wears a wide-brimmed hat and carries a hoe—also a large basket. He looks in.*] Ah! A very charming domestic picture! [*Taking a bunch of radishes from the basket, he speaks to* CHARLOTTE.] My dear, I have found some fine early radishes. I thought it would be a graceful attention on your part to send some of these to Miss de Bourg. [*He sits upon the chair near the doorway.*]

CHARLOTTE.

I fear the apothecary might object.

MR. COLLINS.

True—they might not be suitable, but [*Looking at them proudly.*] they are very fine radishes. [*To* ELIZABETH.] Miss Elizabeth, I am very successful in my gardening. I consider the work I do in my garden to be one of my most respectable pleasures. Lady Catherine is always ready to encourage me in it, and my dear Charlotte is ever willing that I should leave her side for the sake of this healthful exercise. [*Looking at the radishes again.*] It is, indeed, a pity that Miss de Bourg is not well enough to enjoy them. My dear Charlotte has doubtless told you, Miss Elizabeth, of the alliance which is in prospect between Miss de Bourg and Mr. Darcy. This extreme delicacy of constitution would seem to be the only bar to their happiness.

ELIZABETH.

Yes, Charlotte has told me that Miss de Bourg is sickly. She will make Mr. Darcy a very proper wife.

[CHARLOTTE *looks anxiously at* MR. COLLINS *as* ELIZABETH *says this, but he is gazing out of the door and does not seem to notice the remark.*]

MR. COLLINS.

I hope you are pleased with Kent, Miss Elizabeth.

ELIZABETH.

Very much, Mr. Collins.

MR. COLLINS.

I do not think the kingdom can boast a grander scene

than the one now spread before our eyes: [*Pointing.*] This garden—that park with Rosings in the distance. Do not you think my dear Charlotte is most fortunately placed, Miss Elizabeth?

ELIZABETH.

Most fortunately, Mr. Collins.

MR. COLLINS.

And when you have seen Lady Catherine, you will be more deeply impressed, I am sure. We can hardly expect her to call upon you. This illness of Miss de Bourg would prevent it, and in any case it would be an act of extreme condescension on her part; but I am quite confident that you will receive an invitation to drink tea of a Sunday evening with her, after Mr. Darcy and his cousin are gone, of course. And—we may later have an invitation to dinner—although I would not for the world arouse in you false hopes which may be shattered.

MARTHA.

[*Enters in great excitement.*] Oh, Mrs. Collins! Lady Catherine's carriage is turning into the lane and *she* is in it!

MR. COLLINS.

[*Rising in great excitement.*] Lady Catherine—at this hour! What amazing condescension! [*He turns in a helpless manner to* CHARLOTTE.] But, my dear, I am quite unprepared. My habiliments—I would not be wanting in respect.—What shall I do?

CHARLOTTE.

[*Hurriedly putting up her work and giving her hat and gloves to the maid.*] Go make yourself ready, Mr. Collins. We will do the same. [CHARLOTTE *pushes* MR. COLLINS *gently toward the door.*]

MR. COLLINS.

[*Protesting.*] Yes—yes! But this implement—— [*He holds out the hoe.*]

CHARLOTTE.

Give it to Martha!

    [MR. COLLINS *hastily gives the hoe to the maid and then goes out. He instantly returns, however, and again appeals in distressed tones to his wife.*]

MR. COLLINS.

[*Holding out the basket.*] And these radishes, my dear?

CHARLOTTE.

Martha, take the radishes from Mr. Collins.

MARTHA.

Yes, ma'am.

    [*The maid tries to hold at once—basket, hoe, hat, and gloves, as she stands in a corner, open-mouthed.*]

Mr. Collins.

[*Again emerging from the door.*] Do not make yourself uneasy about your own apparel, Miss Elizabeth; Lady Catherine is far from requiring that elegance in us which becomes herself and daughter—I——

Charlotte.

[*Impatiently.*] Oh, do go, Mr. Collins! Lady Catherine will be here in an instant!

[*She shuts the door on* Mr. Collins.]

Elizabeth.

[*Greatly amused at all this excitement.*] Are you going to make any change in your dress, Charlotte? Do you wish me to do so?

Charlotte.

Well, Eliza, if you wouldn't mind, I should like you to put on your sprigged muslin. In spite of what Mr. Collins says, I know it would please him. I have no time to change. Is my cap straight? Oh, here she is. [*To the maid, who stands staring, with her arms full.*] Why, Martha! Are you still there? Go! Go! [*She bustles the maid out of one door, then runs to the other, calling her husband.*] Mr. Collins! Mr. Collins!

> [*She then rushes into the garden, followed immediately by* Mr. Collins *in the same state of excitement.* Elizabeth, *as she looks after them, is convulsed with laughter.*]

Elizabeth.

So, at last—her high and only mightiness! No tremors, Elizabeth! Now is the time for all your courage. [*She runs laughing out of the room.*]

> [*Sounds of voices are heard, and* Lady Catherine *appears escorted up the path by* Charlotte *and* Collins.]

Lady Catherine.

[*As she reaches the door.*] You keep too many hens, Mrs. Collins. There is just a certain number which are profitable—beyond that there is waste. [Lady Catherine *sits on the sofa.*] A clergyman's wife should set an example of thrift. You should have asked my advice.

Mr. Collins.

Mrs. Collins will in the future regulate her poultry-yard according to your directions, Lady Catherine, if you will be so condescending as to give them.

Charlotte.

Yes, thank you, Lady Catherine.

Mr. Collins.

Will your Ladyship not take some refreshment?

Charlotte.

Oh, yes—let me fetch you a cup of tea?

Lady Catherine.

No, no—I wish nothing. [*To* Mr. Collins.] But you may go, Mr. Collins, and see if Jones is walking the horses up and down. I do not trust Jones.

Mr. Collins.

With great pleasure, your Ladyship. [Mr. Collins *goes out.*]

Lady Catherine.

[*To* Charlotte.] I thought you had a visitor, Mrs. Collins.

Charlotte.

Yes, your Ladyship—I have. It is my friend, Miss Elizabeth Bennet. She is a cousin of Mr. Collins and a neighbour of ours in Hertfordshire.

Lady Catherine.

I have heard about her. Fitzwilliam says she is a very genteel, pretty kind of girl.

Charlotte.

[*Pleased.*] Indeed she is, Lady Catherine.

Lady Catherine.

Well, where is she?

Charlotte.

She has gone to make a little change in her dress, before presenting herself to your Ladyship.

LADY CATHERINE.
Oh! very proper—very proper!

CHARLOTTE.
I am delighted to hear that Miss de Bourg is better, Lady Catherine.

LADY CATHERINE.
Yes, thank you. She is very greatly improved. [*After a slight pause, with impatience.*] Well, Miss Bennet takes her time!

CHARLOTTE.
[*Anxiously.*] I am sure she will be here in a moment. [ELIZABETH *enters.*] Oh, here she is. [*Presenting* ELIZABETH.] Lady Catherine, Miss Elizabeth Bennet. [ELIZABETH *curtsies.*]

LADY CATHERINE.
[*Without leaving her seat, looks* ELIZABETH *over from head to foot.*] Oh, how do you do, Miss Bennet. You are younger than I thought!

ELIZABETH.
[*Smiling.*] Indeed?

LADY CATHERINE.
You know my nephew, Mr. Darcy?

ELIZABETH.
Yes, I met him in Hertfordshire.

LADY CATHERINE.
Humph! And you know Colonel Fitzwilliam?

ELIZABETH.
I have only met Colonel Fitzwilliam since coming here.

LADY CATHERINE.
Humph! Has your governess left you?

ELIZABETH.
[*Half laughs.*] My sisters and I have never had a governess, Madam.

LADY CATHERINE.
No governess! I never heard of such a thing! Your mother must have been quite a slave to your education.

ELIZABETH.
[*Smiling.*] I assure you she was not, Lady Catherine.

LADY CATHERINE.
Then who taught you? Without a governess you must have been neglected.

ELIZABETH.
Such of us as wished to learn, never wanted the means, Madam.

LADY CATHERINE.
Well, if I had known your mother, I should have ad-

vised her most strenuously to engage a governess. I should have seen to it myself. [*To* CHARLOTTE.] Go on with your work, Mrs. Collins. A clergyman's wife should set an example of industry. [*Looking at* CHARLOTTE'*s embroidery with disapproval.*] I will send you some more of the parish petticoats to hem, Mrs. Collins. [*To* ELIZABETH.] Go on with your work, Miss Bennet. Young ladies should never be idle. [*Both* ELIZABETH *and* CHARLOTTE *go on with their embroidery. Looking hard at* ELIZABETH.] Pray what is your age, Miss Bennet?

ELIZABETH.
I am not one and twenty.

LADY CATHERINE.
You have sisters, have not you?

ELIZABETH.
Yes, Madam.

LADY CATHERINE.
Are any of them out?

ELIZABETH.
All, Madam.

LADY CATHERINE.
What! All out at once? Very odd! Out before the oldest is married!

Elizabeth.

Really, Madam, I think it would be very hard on the younger sisters not to have their share of society because the eldest one does not happen to be married. That would hardly be likely to promote sisterly affection, or delicacy of mind.

Lady Catherine.

Upon my word, you give your opinion very decidedly for so young a person! Your sisters may be married before you. You must not be too ambitious. A good many young girls have lost their chances through being too ambitious. [*Looking at a large picture on the wall and then pointing to it.*] Mrs. Collins, I suppose you have shown Miss Bennet this print of Pemberley—Mr. Darcy's place?

Charlotte.

Yes, Lady Catherine.

Lady Catherine.

[*Complacently.*] Pemberley is one of the finest places in England. My daughter Anne is very fond of it, which is fortunate, since she will probably spend the most of her life there.

Charlotte.

Most fortunate, your Ladyship.

Lady Catherine.

[*To* Elizabeth.] You see my nephews here often, Miss Bennet?

Elizabeth.

[*Mischievously.*] Yes, *very* often, Lady Catherine.

Lady Catherine.

Humph! Well, idle young gentlemen often make very foolish use of their time. My daughter, Miss de Bourg, is unfortunately not able to accompany Mr. Darcy in his walks as often as both of them could desire.

Mr. Collins.

[*Entering.*] I think your Ladyship's mind may be quite at rest about the horses. Jones seems to have them well in hand.

Lady Catherine.

Oh, I am glad you have come back, Mr. Collins. I am going to ask you and Mrs. Collins to go and see the new cottages with me. I shall take you in the carriage. [*To* Charlotte.] You had better put on a plain bonnet, Mrs. Collins.

Charlotte.

By all means, your Ladyship. [*She goes out.*]

Lady Catherine.

Are you quite ready to go, Mr. Collins?

Mr. Collins.

Oh—assuredly, your Ladyship—quite!

Lady Catherine.

[*To* Elizabeth.] Miss Bennet, I should advise you to

write to your family while we are gone. [CHARLOTTE *returns in her bonnet and mantle.* LADY CATHERINE *looks her over.*] Yes, that will do very well!

CHARLOTTE.

[*To* ELIZABETH.] We shall not be gone very long, Eliza.

LADY CATHERINE.

I am not sure of that, Mrs. Collins, but I have provided an occupation for Miss Bennet during our absence. Good morning, Miss Bennet. I may ask you later for dinner.

ELIZABETH.

[*Curtsying.*] Good morning, Madam. [*All go out,* MR. COLLINS *showing servile attentions to* LADY CATHERINE. ELIZABETH *watches them from the door.*] Really! I might have spared myself some of the mortifications I have felt for the shortcomings of my own family. The contrast is not such a violent one after all. [*Looking at the writing desk.*] However, Lady Catherine can give good advice. I really ought to write to my poor, dear Jane.

[*She seats herself at the writing table—gets out her paper, etc. and begins her letter when the door-bell sounds.* ELIZABETH *starts and is putting away the writing materials, when the maid ushers in* MR. DARCY, *who seems much excited.*]

DARCY.

I am here again, Miss Bennet. I saw Mr. and Mrs.

Collins drive away with my aunt. I have something which I *must* say to you. [*He walks excitedly up and down for a moment, while* ELIZABETH *watches him in amazed silence. Then he suddenly goes up to her and begins to speak in an agitated manner.*] Miss Bennet—in vain have I struggled! It will not do! My feelings will not be repressed! You must allow me to tell you how ardently I admire and love you!

ELIZABETH.
[*Is perfectly astounded. She stares, colours, doubts, and is silent.*]

DARCY.
[*Taking her silence for encouragement.*] Miss Bennet, I can well understand your own astonishment at this declaration, for I am amazed at myself! My feeling for you has taken possession of me against my will, my reason, and almost against my character!

ELIZABETH.
[*Starting in indignation.*] Sir!

DARCY.
Oh, understand me, I beg of you! For yourself alone my admiration is only too natural. I share it with everyone who has the happiness of knowing you. But—pardon me—for it pains me to offend you—the defects of your nearest relations, the total lack of propriety so frequently betrayed by your family, has so opposed my judgment to

my inclination, that it has required the utmost force of passion on my part to put them aside. But, my dear Miss Bennet, your triumph is complete. Your own loveliness stands out the fairer in its contrast to your surroundings, and I now hope that the strength of my love may have its reward in your acceptance of my hand.

Elizabeth.

[*Who has gone through all sorts of emotions during this speech, speaks, in a constrained manner as if trying to control herself.*] Mr. Darcy—in such cases as this, it is, I believe, the established mode to express a sense of obligation for the sentiments avowed, however unequally they may be returned. If I could feel gratitude I would now thank you. But I cannot. I have never desired your good opinion, and *you* have certainly bestowed it most unwillingly.

Darcy.

[*Leaning against the mantel-piece, hears her words with no less resentment than surprise. After a little he speaks in a voice of forced calmness.*] And that is all the reply which I am to have the honour of expecting? I might perhaps wish to be informed why, with so little endeavour at civility, I am thus rejected. But it is of small importance.

Elizabeth.

I might as well inquire why, with so evident a design of insulting me, you chose to tell me that you liked me against your will, your reason, and even against your character! Was not this some excuse for incivility, if I was uncivil?

####### DARCY.

I very clearly explained that the objections which appealed to my reason applied entirely to your *family*, and in no respect to yourself.

####### ELIZABETH.

I am a part of my family, Mr. Darcy; and allow me to say that, since I have had the opportunity of comparing my relations with your own, the contrast is not so marked as I had been led to suppose. [DARCY *starts.*] But—aside from all questions of either feeling or family—do you think any consideration would tempt me to accept the man who has been the means of ruining, perhaps forever, the happiness of a most beloved sister, and involving her in misery of the acutest kind? [DARCY *looks at her with a smile of incredulity.*] Can you deny that you have done this?

####### DARCY.

I have no wish of denying that I did everything in my power to separate my friend from your sister. I did not, indeed, anticipate that I should involve either of them in "misery" of any kind. On your sister's side, at least, I was never able to discover any symptoms of peculiar regard for Mr. Bingley. While, for every reason, I must rejoice in my success with my friend; toward him I have been kinder than toward myself.

Elizabeth.

[*With disdain.*] Your arrogance in calmly deciding the extent of other people's sentiments does not surprise me. It is of a piece with your whole nature! But your interference in my sister's concerns is not all. Long before it had taken place, my opinion of you was decided. Your character was unfolded in the recital which I received months ago from Mr. Wickham. [Darcy *starts excitedly.*] What can you have to say on this subject? In what imaginary act of friendship can you here defend yourself?

Darcy.

[*In a tone of suppressed excitement, in marked contrast to his previous self-assured manner.*] You take an eager interest in that gentleman.

Elizabeth.

Who that knows what his misfortunes have been can help feeling an interest in him?

Darcy.

[*Contemptuously.*] His misfortunes! Yes, his misfortunes have been great indeed!

Elizabeth.

[*With energy.*] And of your infliction! You have reduced him to his present state of poverty—comparative poverty; you have withheld the advantages which you must know to have been designed for him. You have done all this, and yet you can treat the mention of his misfortunes with contempt and ridicule!

Darcy.

[*Walking up and down the room with quick steps.*] And this is your opinion of me? This is the estimation in which you hold me! I thank you for explaining it so fully. [*Stopping and looking at her.*] Perhaps if I were to divulge the truth regarding Mr. Wickham, I might give *you* as great a surprise as you have given *me*. [*After a slight pause.*] I do not care to go into particulars, but in justice to myself, I must tell you that the man whom you consider a martyr is a profligate with the most vicious propensities. A man who should never have entered your home, for his presence there is a constant source of danger.

Elizabeth.

[*In indignation.*] Mr. Darcy!

Darcy.

[*With dignity.*] I am ready to give you the full proofs of all I have said, Miss Bennet, whenever you may so desire, although I would gladly forget all the miserable circumstances myself, and no obligation less than the present should induce me to unfold them to any human being.

Elizabeth.

[*Coldly.*] Your judgment in the matter of my sister's happiness has given me a gauge by which I can measure your fairness to a man who has been so unfortunate as to offend you. My faith in Mr. Wickham is unshaken.

DARCY.

[*Looking at* ELIZABETH *in indignation and by a great effort governing himself.*] I shall take what you have said, Miss Bennet, as a reflection on my *judgment* alone; otherwise, my veracity would be at stake, and this, I am sure, you did not intend. Indeed I understand your whole position perfectly. I have erred in the manner of my declaration. Your bitter accusations might have been suppressed, had I concealed my struggles. It is my own fault. I have wounded your pride. I should have flattered you into the belief that I was impelled by inclination, by reason, by reflection, by everything! But. disguise of every sort is my abhorrence. Could you expect me to rejoice in the inferiority of your connections?

ELIZABETH.

[*Angrily.*] And do you expect *me* to rejoice in your proposal that I ally myself to the conceit and impertinence of *yours?* No, Mr. Darcy! The manner of your declaration has affected me only in one way:—it has spared me the concern which I might otherwise have felt in refusing you, had you behaved in a more *gentlemanlike* way. [DARCY *starts.*] You could not, however, have made me the offer of your hand in any possible way that would have tempted me to accept it. [DARCY *looks at her with an expression of mortified amazement.*] I had not known you a month, before I felt that you were the last man in the world whom I could ever be prevailed upon to marry.

DARCY.

You have said quite enough, Madam! I perfectly comprehend your feelings and have now only to be ashamed of what my own have been. Forgive me for having taken up so much of your time, and accept my best wishes for your health and happiness. [DARCY *hastily leaves the room.*]

ELIZABETH.

[*Sinking into a chair, then getting up and walking excitedly about the room.*] To insult my family! To think I was ready to fall on my knees, in gratitude for his condescension! To calmly dispose of Jane's happiness! [*Stopping in her walk and with a half-amused smile.*] And yet really to be in love with me in spite of every obstacle. [*Throwing herself again into the chair, half laughing, half crying.*] Oh, Jane, Jane! I wish you were here!

MARTHA.

[*Enters with a letter.*] Here is a letter, Miss. The express has just brought it.

ELIZABETH.

A letter? For me?

MAID.

Yes, Miss—[*She gives* ELIZABETH *the letter; curtsies and goes out.*]

ELIZABETH.

[*Looking at the letter.*] Why, it is from Jane! What can be the matter? [*She opens the letter hurriedly and reads.*] "Dearest Lizzy—I have bad news for you, and it cannot be delayed. An express came to us last night from Colonel Forster. He told us that Lydia had run away from Brighton with one of his officers:—to own the truth—with Wickham!

ELIZABETH.

Oh! Wickham! [*Going on with the letter.*] "He first thought they had gone to Scotland, but, oh, Lizzy, it is far worse than that! We now know that Wickham never intended to go there, or to marry Lydia at all!"

ELIZABETH.

Oh! [*Reading again.*] "Colonel Forster has been here to-day. He says Wickham is not a man to be trusted! He has left Brighton terribly in debt, and his record is bad in every way. Oh, Lizzy, our distress is very great! My father is going to London with Colonel Forster instantly to try to discover the fugitives. It is hard to ask you to shorten your visit, but we are in such distress that——" [*Darting from her seat.*] Oh where—where is the express? I must write. No—I must go. Oh, Lydia and Wickham! I must go at once! I must send someone for a carriage. [*She rushes to the garden door calling.*] Martha, Martha! The express! [*Suddenly she calls again.*] Oh, Colonel Fitzwilliam, is that you?

Colonel Fitzwilliam.
[*Appearing in the garden.*] What is the matter, Miss Bennet?

Elizabeth.
[*Wildly.*] Oh, Colonel Fitzwilliam—the express—or can you get me a carriage? I have bad news from home. I must return at once and Mr. Collins is away. Will you be so kind? [*She falls, half-fainting, upon a chair near the door.*]

Colonel Fitzwilliam.
[*With concern.*] Certainly, my dear Miss Bennet—of course—but——[*Calling off.*] Darcy, don't wait for me. I can't join you now. Miss Bennet is in distress.

Darcy.
[*Entering.*] Miss Bennet? Good God! What is the matter?

Colonel Fitzwilliam.
Miss Bennet has just had bad news from home. She wishes to return, and desires a carriage.

Darcy.
[*In a decided tone.*] Do you go for the carriage, Fitzwilliam. Get one from the stables. [Fitzwilliam *hesitates.*]

Darcy.
Go. I will remain with Miss Bennet.
[Fitzwilliam *goes out.*]

DARCY.

[*To* ELIZABETH *very gently.*] Shall I call the maid, Miss Bennet? A glass of wine? Shall I get it for you? You are very ill.

ELIZABETH.

[*Hardly able to speak.*] No, I thank you: there is nothing the matter with me. I am quite well. I am only distressed by some dreadful news which I have just received from Longbourn. [*She bursts into tears.*]

DARCY.

[*Helplessly.*] I am sorry, very indeed!

ELIZABETH.

[*After a short silence.*] I have just had a letter from Jane with such *dreadful* news! It cannot be concealed from anyone.

DARCY.

I am grieved, Miss Bennet. Grieved indeed!

ELIZABETH.

Oh, Mr. Darcy, you were right. If I had only believed you! You, and others! But I could not believe it. [*She sobs.*]

DARCY.

[*Greatly moved.*] What is it, my dear Miss Bennet? What has happened?

ELIZABETH.

[*Wildly.*] Oh, I cannot tell it, and yet everyone must know! My sister Lydia—has—has eloped—has thrown herself into the power of—of *Mr. Wickham!* She has no money, nothing that can tempt him to—she is lost forever! [*She sobs again.*]

DARCY.

Good God, Miss Bennet! Your sister and Wickham! Oh, this is *my* fault. I should have realised this danger—I should have spoken. My own wretched experience with this man should have been told.

ELIZABETH.

[*Wonderingly.*] Your experience!

DARCY.

Yes—I—you remember. I hinted it to you—to-day. But I should long ago have spoken boldly.

ELIZABETH.

What do you mean?

DARCY.

Mr. Wickham attempted this same plan with my own sister—two years ago. She was an ignorant, innocent, trusting girl of fifteen. Happily, his villainy was discovered and prevented. But oh, I should have told you! Had his character been known, this could not have happened.

ELIZABETH.

You tried to tell me, Mr. Darcy. Everybody has tried to warn me. But I could not believe it, and now—it is too late, too late!

DARCY.

Let us hope not. Is what you have told me certain—absolutely certain?

ELIZABETH.

Oh, yes. They left Brighton together on Sunday night. They are certainly not gone to Scotland.

DARCY.

And what has been done, or attempted, to recover your sister?

ELIZABETH.

My father has gone to London. He will beg my uncle Gardiner's assistance. But nothing *can* be done! I know very well that nothing can be done. How is such a man to be worked on? How are they ever to be discovered? I have not the smallest hope. It is all horrible!

DARCY.

Miss Bennet, I have made a wretched mistake in all this. Would to Heaven that anything could be said or done on my part that might make you reparation, or offer consolation to such distress!

[ELIZABETH *sinks sobbing into a chair while* DARCY *walks up and down in deep thought. In a moment a carriage is heard outside—then voices.*]

Darcy.

[*Looking out.*] Mr. and Mrs. Collins are returning. What would you wish me to do?

Elizabeth.

Oh, I do not know! I do not know!

Darcy.

[*Returning to* Elizabeth, *speaks quickly and in deep concern.*] You really wish to return home at once?

Elizabeth.

[*Rising from her chair.*] Oh, yes, yes—at once. [*Reaching her hand to him appealingly.*] Take me home, Mr. Darcy! Take me home!

> [*At this instant* Mr. *and* Mrs. Collins *appear at the garden door, and, transfixed with astonishment, stand gazing at* Darcy *and* Elizabeth.]

ACT IV

ACT IV

The Lawn and Shrubbery at Longbourn. MRS. BENNET *is seated in a garden chair with pillows at her back. She has an umbrella over her head. Near her stands a table on which are bottles, dishes, etc. She wears a big cap, and is gowned in a widely-flowing, flowered chamber-robe, over which is fastened a shawl; across her knees is a lap-robe. Her entire get-up is grotesque and laughable. About her hover the housekeeper,* HILL *and* JANE.

JANE.

Dear mamma, do try and take some of this nice gruel. You will be ill if you do not eat something.

HILL.

Yes, do, I beg of you, Madam. Now that you are once more in the air, if you will only take some food you will feel much better.

MRS. BENNET.

[*Fretfully.*] How can I feel better? I must be ill. It is all very well for the rest of you, now that this disgrace has been brought upon me—but if I had been able to carry my point—if I could have gone to Brighton with all my family, this would never have happened. But poor dear

Lydia had nobody to take care of her. Oh, that villainous Wickham! I am sure there was some great neglect or other somewhere, for Lydia is not the kind of girl to run away with a man. But no one would listen to me. I was overruled, as I always am. Poor Lydia! Poor dear child!

Jane.
[*Soothingly.*] Oh, mamma, try to be calm.

Hill.
Yes, Madam, this excitement is so bad for you.

Mrs. Bennet.
How can I help being excited? You have no feelings. Here is Mr. Bennet gone away, and I know he will fight that abominable Wickham and be killed. And then what is to become of us all? The Collinses will turn us out before Mr. Bennet is cold in his grave.

Jane.
Oh, mamma, do not have such terrific ideas.

Mrs. Bennet.
[*Weeping.*] If my brother Gardiner is not kind to me, I do not know what we shall do.

Jane.
Yes, yes. My Uncle Gardiner is very kind. He is doing everything in his power for us. He is helping my

father now in London, you know. I hope he will find Lydia, and perhaps he may be able to arrange a marriage after all. You must not give up so, dear mamma.

HILL.

No indeed, Madam. You must not indeed.

MRS. BENNET.

[*Brightening.*] Yes, Jane, that is true. My brother may be able to see that they are married. Write to him at once, Jane. Tell him to find them out wherever they may be, and if they are not married already, make them marry. Oh, I do think that Wickham is the wickedest young man in the world to so deceive my poor innocent Lydia. But, Jane, go and write my brother and tell him that Lydia need not wait for wedding clothes—don't let her even give directions till she has seen me, for she doesn't know which are the best warehouses. And oh, Jane, tell my brother to keep your father from fighting that hateful Wickham. Tell him what a dreadful state I am in.

JANE.

Yes, mamma. [*She is about to go.*]

MRS. BENNET.

Where are you going?

JANE.

Why, to write the letter, mamma.

MRS. BENNET.

[*Fretfully.*] Oh, not just this minute. Don't leave me alone. Where is Lizzy?

JANE.

She has gone down the road to meet the post. She hopes to bring you good news.

MRS. BENNET.

[*Lamenting.*] She had better stay here and be of some help. She has only just got home and now she leaves me. But nobody thinks of me. Nobody knows what I suffer. I am frightened out of my wits. I have such tremblings and flutterings all over me—such spasms in my side—and pains in my head, and such beatings at my heart. Oh, I can get no rest by night or by day! [*To* HILL.] You might try and do something, Hill. Where is my soothing draught?

HILL.

[*Looking.*] Here, Madam. No, I must have left it in your room. I will run fetch it. [*She goes out quickly.*]

JANE.

[*Who has been looking off toward the driveway during part of this tirade.*] Oh, mamma—mamma! Lizzy's running up the drive. She is smiling! She has some good news, I am sure.

MRS. BENNET.

Take care, Jane. You are exciting me. Oh, my poor nerves.

[ELIZABETH *enters, breathless. She has a letter in her hand.*]

ELIZABETH.

Oh, good news—good news, Jane!—mamma! They are married!

JANE.

Oh, Lizzy—Lizzy!

MRS. BENNET.

You are sure, Lizzy? Don't excite me. You are sure?

ELIZABETH.

[*Half laughing and half crying.*] Oh, yes, 'tis certain. My dear Aunt Gardiner has written me all about it. They are really married! Oh, how good my uncle is! [*She kisses the letter.*]

MRS. BENNET.

Oh, Jane—Oh, Lizzy! My dear, dear Lydia! She is really married! I shall see her again! Oh, my good, kind brother! But how did it happen, Lizzy?

JANE.

Yes, tell us all about it. Let me read it. [*She reaches for the letter.*]

ELIZABETH.

[*Keeping the letter.*] No, I will tell you. Well, my father and my uncle succeeded in finding Lydia. My aunt does not tell me just how it was done.

MRS. BENNET.

[*Triumphantly.*] And your father found that they were married after all. I told him——

ELIZABETH.

No, mamma. They were not married, and they had no idea of being—but my father and uncle insisted upon it. They took Lydia away at once to my aunt's house and from there, they were married only yesterday at St. Clement's Church.

MRS. BENNET.

St. Clement's—fine!

ELIZABETH.

My dear good uncle has arranged to have all Mr. Wickham's debts paid and my father is to settle an allowance on Lydia.

JANE.

But where are they? What are they going to do?

ELIZABETH.

My father is coming home at once. He may be here at any moment. At first he would not consent to let Lydia and Wickham come to us, but my aunt and uncle urged it—and my father knew how anxious mamma would be—and so *they* are coming here too.

JANE.

At once?

ELIZABETH.

Yes, directly, to-day.

MRS. BENNET.

Oh, my dear Lydia! How I long to see her, and to see my dear Wickham too. But the clothes, the wedding clothes! I must write to my Sister Gardiner about them directly.

[*She tries to get out of the chair.*]

JANE.

Oh, mamma, there is plenty of time for that.

MRS. BENNET.

Well, perhaps so. My dear, dear Lydia! How merry we shall all be together! I am so happy! Lydia married. She is Mrs. Wickham. How well it sounds. My dear Jane, I must see about the clothes. We will settle with your father about the money later. Oh, I am in such a flutter! Here comes Hill. [HILL *enters with the bottle.*] My dear Hill, have you heard the news? Miss Lydia is married and is coming home directly.

HILL.

Indeed!

Mrs. Bennet.

Yes, you shall all have a bowl of punch, to make merry for her wedding, and I am going into the house to write about the clothes. [*To* Jane, *who is going with her.*] No, Jane, you stay where you are. I know what I am about. Come, Hill. Think of it—Mrs. Wickham!

[*She goes out leaning on* Hill's *arm, leaving* Jane *and* Elizabeth *together.*]

Jane.

Oh, Lizzy, how relieved and happy we should be. Is not it wonderful? [*Anxiously.*] Are you sure it is true? Have you told us all?

Elizabeth.

Yes, Jane, it is true. They are really married. And for this we are to be thankful. In spite of Lydia's folly and Wickham's wretched character, we are to rejoice. How strange it is! Heigh-ho!

Jane.

[*Putting out her hand for the letter which* Elizabeth *still carries.*] May not I read the letter, Lizzy?

Elizabeth.

No, not now, dear. My aunt has some queer notions in her head. Later perhaps. [*After a pause.*] I am very sorry now that in my agitation I told Mr. Darcy about this wretched affair. Now that it has come out so well, he need never have known anything about it, and it would have saved me a great deal of mortification.

JANE.

But how would you ever have explained things to Charlotte and Mr. Collins without his help? Mr. Darcy made everything so smooth and plausible for your sudden departure.

ELIZABETH.

Yes, that is true.

JANE.

Really, Lizzy, I think I shall have to take up the cudgels in Mr. Darcy's defence. His kindness to you has quite won my heart, and his amazing proposal was certainly a most flattering compliment. Why can you see no good in Mr. Darcy, Lizzy? You were always so full of excuses for Wickham, though it is true his open and delightful manners deceived us all.

ELIZABETH.

Yes, there certainly was some great mismanagement in the education of those two young men. One has all the goodness and the other all the appearance of it.

JANE.

I never thought Mr. Darcy so deficient in the appearance of it as you did, and he certainly could hardly have had the friends he has if he did not possess some good qualities.

[*Shyly.*] Lizzy, have you heard that Mr. Bingley is back in Netherfield?

ELIZABETH.

[*Astonished.*] Oh, Jane, no. When did he come? Have you seen him?

JANE.

No; I hardly expect to see him.

ELIZABETH.

[*Brightly.*] Yes, you will, if he has returned. [*Suddenly clapping her hands.*] Oh, I understand. [*Kissing her.*] My darling Jane, you are going to be very happy!

JANE.

Lizzy dear—don't, don't. That is all over now, and besides I don't want to be happy unless you can be, too.

ELIZABETH.

Oh, forty Mr. Bingleys wouldn't make me happy. Till I have your disposition, I never can have happiness. No, no, let me shift for myself. Perhaps if I have very good luck I may meet with another Mr. Collins in time.

HARRIS.

[*Entering.*] Mr. Bennet has returned, Madam, and is looking for you.

JANE.

Papa returned!

ELIZABETH.

Where is he, Harris? [*Looking off.*] There he comes! Papa!

[*They run to meet* MR. BENNET, *and, bringing him in, seat him in a garden chair, one on either side of him.*]

ELIZABETH.

Papa, tell us all about it quickly—quickly.

JANE.

Are they really married, papa?

MR. BENNET.

Yes, that misfortune is well settled on them. They are married fast enough.

ELIZABETH.

And where are they? When will they be here?

MR. BENNET.

I should say they would be here directly. I didn't care to travel with them, but they are not far behind—only just far enough to keep out of the dust of my post chaise.

ELIZABETH.

Dear papa—how you must have suffered!

MR. BENNET.

Say nothing of that—who should suffer but myself? It has been my own doing, and I ought to feel it.

ELIZABETH.
You must not be too severe upon yourself.

MR. BENNET.
You may well warn me against such an evil. No, Lizzy, let me once in my life feel how much I have been to blame. The impression will pass away soon enough.

ELIZABETH.
But, papa, how did you persuade them to marry?

MR. BENNET.
I didn't persuade them; I haven't the means. It is all your uncle's doing. He has managed to buy Wickham for us.

JANE.
Oh, dear good uncle!

MR. BENNET.
[*Looks at* JANE *quizzically.*] But there are two things that I want very much to know—one is how much money your uncle has laid down to bring it about, and the other, how I am ever to pay him.

JANE.
But my uncle did not do it all?

ELIZABETH.
No, papa. My Aunt Gardiner has written me that you are to give Lydia an allowance.

MR. BENNET.

Yes, one hundred a year. Do you think that any man in his proper senses would marry Lydia on so slight a temptation as one hundred a year?

ELIZABETH.

That is very true, though it had not occurred to me before. Oh, it must be my uncle's doings. Generous man! I am afraid he has distressed himself. A small sum could not do all this.

MR. BENNET.

No, Wickham's a fool if he takes Lydia with a farthing less than ten thousand pounds. I should be sorry to think so ill of him in the very beginning of our relationship.

ELIZABETH.

Ten thousand pounds! Heaven forbid! How is one-half such a sum to be repaid?

MR. BENNET.
That is what I should like to know.

ELIZABETH.

Well, my uncle's kindness can never be requited. If such goodness as his does not make Lydia miserable, then she will never deserve to be happy.

[*Laughter and voices are heard outside.*]

ELIZABETH.

Surely I hear voices. [*Looking off.*] Why, they have come. See papa—Jane—there are Lydia and Wickham.

MR. BENNET.

Yes, here they are. I will go to the library. I can receive their congratulations later. You know I am prodigiously fond of Wickham, Lizzy. I defy even Sir William Lucas himself to produce a more valuable son-in-law.
[*He goes out.*]

JANE.

I must run and tell mamma.
> [*She is just starting when* WICKHAM *and* LYDIA *enter. They are in travelling dress and are followed by servants bringing all sorts of bandboxes, wraps and parcels. They come in with the utmost unconcern and no shadow of shame.*]

LYDIA.

Well, Jane, well, Lizzy, here we are!

WICKHAM.

[*Smiling and unabashed.*] My sister, Jane—My sister Elizabeth.
> [*He kisses their hands.* JANE *and* ELIZABETH *are confused and blushing. Neither* WICKHAM *nor* LYDIA *is in the least discomposed.*]

LYDIA.

[*Looking about.*] Good gracious! Here I am again! I am sure I had no idea of being married when I went away, though I thought it would be very good fun if I was. Why don't you take the boxes in, Harris? Wickham, have you seen my pink-flowered bandbox? [*Looking over the parcels.*] No, it isn't here. Oh, my dear Wickham, do go fetch it—you know 'tis the box with the white satin hat you bought me. I wouldn't lose it for the world. Go, go!

WICKHAM.

Certainly, my dear. [*To the girls.*] You see how eagerly I embrace my new opportunities!

[*He runs out, laughing.*]

LYDIA.

[*To* ELIZABETH *and* JANE.] Oh, girls, I am dying to give you an account of my wedding.

ELIZABETH.

I think there cannot be too little said on that subject.

LYDIA.

La, you are so strange. But Jane wants to hear, I know. Anyway, I want to tell you. Well, there was such a fuss! My aunt was preaching and talking away to me all the time I was dressing, just as if she was reading a sermon. I didn't hear one word in ten of it all. I was thinking of my dear Wickham. I longed to know whether he would be married in his blue coat. Well, we got to church, and then my uncle gave me a fright after we got there, because he was so late, and he was going to give me away, you know. But then, if he hadn't come, Mr. Darcy might have done as well.

Jane and Elizabeth.

Mr. Darcy!

Lydia.

Oh, yes, Darcy was there. He came along with Wickham. [*Suddenly stopping.*] But gracious me! I quite forgot. I ought not to have said a word about it. I promised them as faithfully—what will Wickham say? It was to be such a secret.

Jane.

If it was to be a secret, Lydia, say not another word on the subject. We shall ask you no questions.

[Elizabeth *looks most anxious, but says nothing.*]

Lydia.

Thank you—for if you did, I should certainly tell you all, and then Wickham would be angry. [*She sees* Mrs. Bennet, *who enters in great excitement from the house.*] Oh, there is mamma.

[*They rush into each other's arms.* Wickham *returns at about the same time.*]

MRS. BENNET.

Oh, my dear, dear Lydia! [*To* WICKHAM *with affectionate warmth.*] My dear Wickham!
[*They also embrace.*]

LYDIA.

Oh, mamma! Aren't you glad to see us? [WICKHAM *turns and talks to* JANE *and* ELIZABETH.] Do all the people hereabouts know that I am married? I was afraid they might not, and so I let my hand just rest on the window-frame outside the carriage, so that everybody could see my wedding ring; and then I bowed and smiled like everything.

MRS. BENNET.

You may be sure, my dear, that everybody will rejoice with us in our good luck. [*Sighing.*] Your marriage is a great compensation to me after all my disappointment about Jane and Lizzy. I do not blame Jane, for she would have got Mr. Bingley if she could. But Lizzy! Oh, Lydia, it is very hard to think she might now have been Mrs. Collins! But how about your clothes?

LYDIA.

Oh, I have a lot already. You may be sure I would not forget *them*.

MRS. BENNET.

[*Alarmed.*] But you didn't know the best warehouses! Well, never mind, we will see to that later. Now you must all come in and have dinner. You must be famished. Come, girls. Come, my dear Wickham.

[*They all go toward the house. At the door* LYDIA *pushes* JANE *back.*]

LYDIA.

Ah, Jane, I take your place now. I go first because I am a married woman.

[*They all go into the house. After a pause,* HARRIS'S *voice is heard outside.*]

HARRIS.

Will not you come into the house, Madam?

LADY CATHERINE.

[*Entering, followed by* HARRIS.] No, I prefer to remain here. Tell Miss Elizabeth Bennet that a lady wishes to see her at once. Remember, I cannot be kept waiting.

HARRIS.

Yes, Madam. [*He bows and goes out.*]

LADY CATHERINE.

[*Looks about her with a sniff, then deliberately seats herself in the big garden chair with the umbrella over it. She mutters to herself from time to time and taps her foot impatiently.*] Insufferable impudence! Conceited little minx! She shall have a piece of my mind.

[ELIZABETH *comes to her from the house.*]

LADY CATHERINE.

[*Without moving.*] Miss Bennet, you can be at no loss to understand the reason of my journey hither. Your own heart—your own conscience must tell you why I come.

ELIZABETH.

[*In unaffected astonishment.*] Indeed, you are mistaken, Madam. I am not at all able to account for the honour of seeing you here.

LADY CATHERINE.

Miss Bennet, you ought to know that I am not to be trifled with. I have just been told that you—that Miss Elizabeth Bennet would in all likelihood be soon married to my nephew, Mr. Darcy. Though I know it to be a scandalous falsehood, I instantly resolved on setting off for this place that I might make my sentiments known to you.

ELIZABETH.

[*With astonishment and disdain.*] If you believed it impossible to be true, I wonder you took the trouble of coming so far. What could your Ladyship propose by it?

LADY CATHERINE.

At once to insist upon having such a report universally contradicted.

ELIZABETH.

[*Coolly.*] Your coming to Longbourn to see me and my

family, will be rather a confirmation of it, if indeed such a report is in existence.

####### LADY CATHERINE.
If! Do you then pretend to be ignorant of it? Do you not know that such a report is spread about?

####### ELIZABETH.
I never heard that it was.

####### LADY CATHERINE.
And can you likewise declare that there is no foundation for it?

####### ELIZABETH.
Your Ladyship may ask questions which I shall not choose to answer.

####### LADY CATHERINE.
This is not to be borne. Miss Bennet, I insist upon being satisfied. Has he—has my nephew made you an offer of marriage?

####### ELIZABETH.
Your Ladyship has declared it to be impossible.

####### LADY CATHERINE.
It ought to be so. But your arts and allurements may have made him forget what he owes to himself and to all his family. You may have drawn him in.

Elizabeth.

If I have, I shall be the last person to confess it.

Lady Catherine.

Miss Bennet, do you know who I am? I have not been accustomed to such language as this. I am Mr. Darcy's own aunt, and am entitled to know all his dearest concerns.

Elizabeth.

But you are not entitled to know *mine*.

Lady Catherine.

Let me be rightly understood. This match can never take place. No, never. Mr. Darcy is engaged to my daughter. Now what have you got to say?

Elizabeth.

Only this—that if it is so, you can have no reason to suppose Mr. Darcy will make an offer to me.

Lady Catherine.

[*Hesitating.*] The engagement between them is of a peculiar kind. While in their cradles, my sister and I planned their union. Do you pay no regard to the wishes of his friends? Do not you see that honour, decorum—nay, interest, forbid you marrying my nephew? Yes *interest*, Miss Bennet. For you will be slighted and despised by everyone connected with him!

ELIZABETH.

These are heavy misfortunes. But the wife of Mr. Darcy must have such extraordinary sources of happiness that she could have no cause to repine.

LADY CATHERINE.

[*In a rage.*] Obstinate, headstrong girl! Tell me once for all—are you engaged to my nephew?

ELIZABETH.

[*Hesitates, then firmly.*] I am not.

LADY CATHERINE.

[*Relieved.*] And will you promise me never to enter into such an engagement?

ELIZABETH.

I will make no promise of the kind.

LADY CATHERINE.

Miss Bennet, I am shocked and astonished. I shall not go away until you have given me the assurance I require.

ELIZABETH.

And I certainly never shall give it. I must beg, therefore, to be importuned no further on the subject.

LADY CATHERINE.

[*In a fury, but trying to speak calmly.*] Not so hasty, if you please. I had hoped to spare you this last humiliation—but your insolence forbids it. I am no stranger to the particulars of your sister's infamous elopement. I know all! The young man's marrying her was a patched-up business at the expense of *my nephew.* [ELIZABETH *starts violently.*] Oh, you needn't start, Miss! Nobody knows about the whole affair better than you. But I don't wonder you blush to find yourself discovered. You used your arts well. My nephew must have spent full five or six thousand pounds to save your family from disgrace. I should think that such generosity might appeal a little to your gratitude and your sense of decency.

ELIZABETH.
[*Amazed.*] Oh, Madam,—I——

LADY CATHERINE.
It is quite useless to protest. I have my facts from the best authority. Heaven knows Darcy has reason enough to keep away from Wickham's flirtations and entanglements, but [*stopping herself.*] that is a family affair. However, *you* have managed to get him mixed up in them again to the extent of five thousand pounds. But that is not enough,—you want to make this shameless girl my nephew's *sister,* and the son of his father's steward his brother. Heaven and Earth! Are the shades of Pemberley to be thus polluted?

ELIZABETH.
[*Speaking with great effort.*] Madam, you have in-

sulted me in every possible manner. I must beg to return to the house. This is beyond endurance.

LADY CATHERINE.
Selfish girl! You are then resolved to have him?

ELIZABETH.
Lady Catherine, I have nothing further to say.

LADY CATHERINE.
[*Rising from her chair.*] Very well. I shall now know how to act. Do not imagine your ambition will be gratified. Depend upon it, I shall carry my point. [*Going.*] I take no leave of you, Miss Bennet. You deserve no such attention. You will see what it is to rouse my displeasure.

[LADY CATHERINE *goes out.*]

ELIZABETH.
[*Sinking upon the garden seat, overwhelmed.*] Can it be possible? Do we owe all this to Darcy? Oh, it is intolerable! [*She puts her hands over her face in an abandonment of grief.*]

JANE.
[*Is heard outside calling.*] Lizzy! Lizzy! [*She enters, and on seeing her sister rushes to her.*] Lizzy dear! What is it? Is there any new trouble?

ELIZABETH.
[*Throwing her arms about her sister.*] Oh, Jane, Jane!

Yes, there is no end of trouble. Lady Catherine has been here.

JANE.

[*Astounded.*] Lady Catherine!

ELIZABETH.

Yes, yes, and—she says—that—oh, Jane——

JANE.

[*Distressed.*] *Tell* me, Lizzy!

ELIZABETH.

She says it was Darcy who paid all the money to Wickham—it was Darcy saved us—and—and she says I persuaded him. *I* ensnared him, and—and she has insulted me.

JANE.

My dear, dear Lizzy. There *must* be some mistake. It was my good uncle who——

ELIZABETH.

[*A little calmer.*] No—no, Jane, it must be true. I can put things together now. My aunt's hints in the letter—you know I did not want to show it you. Then what Lydia let fall, and her fear of Wickham's anger.

JANE.

[*Soothingly.*] Well, dear, even so, Mr. Darcy's *motive* is clear enough—and that should give you no pain.

ELIZABETH.

You are mistaken. I know his motive. He feels that he is responsible because he was silent about Wickham's true character. He told me that all this would never have happened, had he done his duty. And now, he will despise us. He will never wish to see us again as long as he lives!

[*She walks up and down in great excitement.*]

HARRIS.

[*Entering; to* JANE.] The young gentlemen from Netherfield, Madam. I told them they would find you here.

ELIZABETH.

Oh, Jane, I *cannot* see them.

[*She tries to run away, but before she can escape* BINGLEY *enters, all smiles, followed by* DARCY, *who looks very much troubled and excited. They are both in riding dress;* DARCY *carries a whip.*]

BINGLEY.

[*Shaking hands.*] Miss Bennet, I am so happy to see you again. Miss Elizabeth, it is good indeed to be back once more at Longbourn.

[*He takes* JANE *to a garden seat.*]

DARCY.

[*Embarrassed.*] Miss Bennet, believe me, I should not have followed my friend. I only expected to ride with him to the Lodge, but—but I met my aunt coming away from here, and from something she said, I feared,—I imagined she might have offended—distressed you.

[ELIZABETH *does not reply.*]

BINGLEY.

[*Gaily.*] Miss Bennet is going to show me the Hermitage. We shall be back directly.

[JANE *and* BINGLEY *go out.*]

DARCY.

[*Looking anxiously at* ELIZABETH, *who remains silent.*] Forgive my intrusion. I will go.

[*He starts to go away.*]

ELIZABETH.

[*Recovering herself.*] No—stay, Mr. Darcy. Excuse my own incivility. Your aunt's visit has excited me. I shall be myself in a moment. [DARCY *stands by, miserable. At length she speaks in a calmer tone.*] Mr. Darcy, your aunt has told me of our overwhelming obligation to you. You must let me thank you for your unexampled kindness to my poor sister.

DARCY.

[*Exploding and banging his whip against his knees.*]
Damn!—Oh, I beg your pardon, Miss Bennet. I *beg* your pardon. What right has my aunt to meddle in my affairs? How *dare* she give you such distress?

Elizabeth.

It is far better that we know the truth, Mr. Darcy. For my part, I can never express to you our obligation.

Darcy.

Oh, Miss Bennet—I beg of you! The obligation was entirely my own. I only did what was my decent, plain duty. [*Faltering.*] You remember—I told you—if I had spoken, this would never have happened.

Elizabeth.

Yes, I remember. But you exaggerated your responsibility. I—we—of course my father will see you about your loan to us. I would not have Lady Catherine think——

Darcy.

[*Furious again.*] Oh, I will settle matters with Lady Catherine! Have no fears on that score, Miss Bennet. *She* shall be set right, I assure you.

Elizabeth.

Thank you. And for all your trouble—your kindness—my family can never repay you.

Darcy.

Your family owes me nothing. If I had any thought beyond my duty, it was a thought of—you. [Elizabeth *turns away.*] Oh, pardon me. Perhaps, I ought not to say all this—but I owe you a great deal, Miss Bennet—

more than you can know; and I want you to understand me better. I really am not the pretentious prig I must have seemed to you. I wish you could forgive my abominable pride.

ELIZABETH.

[*Looking at him with a half smile.*] I will, on one condition.

DARCY.

Name it.

ELIZABETH.

That you forget my unwarrantable prejudice.

DARCY.

Oh, Miss Bennet! [*He goes impetuously forward—then restraining himself, smiles and looks down at her.*] I really think, after all, I shall have to be grateful to my aunt. She has done us an enormous service.

ELIZABETH.

[*Smiling still more.*] Well, Lady Catherine loves to be useful!

> [*At the back of the scene* BINGLEY *and* JANE, *absorbed in each other, pass by, hand in hand.* ELIZABETH *looks at them, then turns to* DARCY.]

ELIZABETH.

[*Archly.*] Is *that* by your permission?

DARCY.

[*Ruefully.*] Yes, I told you I had been kinder to my friend than to myself.

> [ELIZABETH, *silent, still looks after* BINGLEY *and* JANE.]

DARCY.

[*Continues in a discouraged tone.*] Well, I deserve it. It is my own fault. My selfish conceit has wounded you past help. Every sentiment of your nature has felt it—seen it.

ELIZABETH.

[*Demurely.*] But *one* sentiment they say is *blind*.

DARCY.

[*Stunned.*] Miss Bennet! [ELIZABETH *looks up at him. He rushes toward her.*] Dearest, loveliest Elizabeth!

> [*He holds her in his arms.*]

CURTAIN.

www.ingramcontent.com/pod-product-compliance
Lightning Source LLC
Chambersburg PA
CBHW030827230426
43667CB00008B/1417